More Praise for *The Resilient Investor*

"This book is brilliant! By redefining and broadening what it means to invest, it helps chart a course toward making the most productive use of both your money and your time and live a more fulfilling life in alignment with your values."
—**Jenny Kassan, CEO, Cutting Edge Capital**

"Today more than ever, investors must cultivate the virtue of resilience. *The Resilient Investor* shows us exactly how to do so with expansive vision, solid money advice, and practical wisdom, establishing beyond a doubt that resilient investors are, in the long run, the most successful investors."
—**Patricia Aburdene, author of *Conscious Money* and *Megatrends 2010***

"This unique original treatment of investing is holistic in the best sense of the word: it connects investing to the rest of your life, brings it down to earth, normalizes it, and offers valuable insights into how you can truly think anew about your money while deploying it mindfully in the service of personal and societal goals."
—**Joe Keefe, President and CEO, Pax World Management LLC**

"*The Resilient Investor* shows how thoughtful investment, in all senses of the word, can both protect and buffer us from an unpredictable and worrisome future. But this book does something even more important: it also shows us how the right investments can influence that future and ensure it is the one we want."
—**Auden Schendler, Vice President of Sustainability, Aspen Skiing Company, and author of *Getting Green Done***

"The global community is headed for increasingly turbulent times with greater risk and volatility. *The Resilient Investor* teaches us how to prepare by considering every aspect of our lives in mapping our future scenarios."
—**Carsten Henningsen, Chairman, Portfolio 21**

"What could be more important, in the world of ultrafast trading, rogue computer algorithms, and climate change, than weaning ourselves off Wall Street? We need to reinvent investing in the 21st century. The thinking that informs this book is a vital part of that urgent process."
—**Woody Tasch, founder and Chairman, Slow Money**

"A timely and refreshing rethink of what it means to invest. *The Resilient Investor* takes the big view, while helping readers create a holistic investment plan that will serve their goals—no matter what the future holds."
—**Amy Cortese, author of *Locavesting***

D0182319

The
Resilient
Investor

A Plan for Your Life,

Not Just Your Money

Hal Brill

Michael Kramer

Christopher Peck

with Jim Cummings

BK

Berrett–Koehler Publishers, Inc.
a BK Life book

Berrett-Koehler Publishers, Inc.
1333 Broadway, Suite 1000, Oakland, CA 94612-1921
Tel: (510) 817-2277   Fax: (510) 817-2278   www.bkconnection.com

This publication contains the authors' opinions and is designed to provide accurate and authoritative information. It is sold with the understanding that the authors, Natural Investments, LLC, and the publisher are not engaged in rendering legal, accounting, investment-planning, or other professional advice. The reader should seek the services of a qualified professional for such advice. The authors, Natural Investments, LLC, and the publisher cannot be held responsible for any loss incurred as a result of specific investments or planning decisions made by the reader.

Ordering Information

Quantity sales. Special discounts are available on quantity purchases by corporations, associations, and others. For details, contact the "Special Sales Department" at the Berrett-Koehler address above.

Individual sales. Berrett-Koehler publications are available through most bookstores. They can also be ordered directly from Berrett-Koehler:
Tel: (800) 929-2929; Fax: (802) 864-7626; www.bkconnection.com.
Orders for college textbook/course adoption use. Please contact Berrett-Koehler:
Tel: (800) 929-2929; Fax: (802) 864-7626.
Orders by U.S. trade bookstores and wholesalers. Please contact Ingram Publisher Services, Tel: (800) 509-4887; Fax: (800) 838-1149; E-mail: customer.service@ ingrampublisherservices.com; or visit www.ingrampublisherservices.com/Ordering for details about electronic ordering.

Berrett-Koehler and the BK logo are registered trademarks of Berrett-Koehler Publishers, Inc.

Printed in the United States of America

Berrett-Koehler books are printed on long-lasting acid-free paper. When it is available, we choose paper that has been manufactured by environmentally responsible processes. These may include using trees grown in sustainable forests, incorporating recycled paper, minimizing chlorine in bleaching, or recycling the energy produced at the paper mill.

Library of Congress Cataloging-in-Publication Data
Brill, Hal, 1956–
    The resilient investor : a plan for your life, not just your money / Hal Brill, Michael Kramer, Christopher Peck ; with Jim Cummings. — First Edition.
        pages cm
    Includes bibliographical references and index.
    ISBN 978-1-62656-337-7 (pbk.)
1. Finance, Personal. 2. Investments—Planning. I. Title.
    HG179.B73193 2015
    332.6—dc23
                                                                    2014040638

19 18 17 16 15   10 9 8 7 6 5 4 3 2 1

Cover design by Brad Foltz. Cover illustration by Vetta/Getty Images.
Interior design and composition by Gary Palmatier, Ideas to Images.
Elizabeth von Radics, copyeditor; Mike Mollett, proofreader; Rachel Rice, indexer.

Contents

Standing Up to Uncertainty

DOES THE CHALLENGE OF MAKING INFORMED DECISIONS ABOUT YOUR life seem far more complex today than it did even a short time ago? Does the future—your own and that of the world—feel highly uncertain, perhaps even precarious?

We can sense you there, nodding in agreement. We would also wager that you would love to have a crystal ball that could tell you how the future will unfold, enabling you to make prescient decisions as you glide through life. Indeed much of today's media aims to quench that thirst for guidance, projecting a steady stream of "experts" onto our screens, each of whom is rife with insight to help us understand how things will unfold. And we lap it up, even though we have seen all too often how their predictions are mocked by the actual turn of events.

So we need to say right at the outset that you've just picked up a book that is *not* going to tell you what's going to happen this year or next. It would certainly be much easier to market a book that reveals our "three smart money secrets"—everyone's a winner! Once in a great while, those sorts of books guess right—but we cannot in good conscience make that pitch for one simple reason: the future has yet to be written. There are no simple formulas that can be relied on in this complex and unpredictable world.

The good news is that this book offers something even more valuable: a dynamic framework that will help you navigate the stormy times in which we live. The tools we offer are designed to keep you nimble, which you'll need to be as the ground continues to shift. Because although we cannot tell you *how* things will change, we do know that they *will* change.

Although humanity has faced immense challenges before, the sense that things really are different this time is one that is shared by the US military. They coined the acronym *VUCA*, which stands for *volatile, uncertain, complex,* and *ambiguous.* Interestingly, they started using this term *before* the 9/11 attacks, superstorms, the financial meltdown, and all the other events that have pummeled us in this fledgling century. At the same time, forward-looking companies have turned the complexity of our times into opportunities; *Fast Company* calls this the Age of Flux, "defined more by fluidity than by any new, settled paradigm. If there's one consistent pattern, it's that there is no pattern."[1]

It is ironic that in these turbulent times, when we most crave a road map to show us where we are going, our visibility into the future is most limited. It's like trying to drive through a thick fog and realizing that no one has invented a fog light that really works and that the maps we have are useless because we cannot see the signs.

Many investors swerved to the side of the road, stopping wherever they were when the fog rolled in. They have bailed on Wall Street but don't have a clue about what to do instead. Even while the Dow was steadily climbing after the crash, individual investors kept yanking money out of stock mutual funds right through 2012.[2] Much of that cash has been parked in today's version of a mattress: bank accounts earning such minuscule interest that they do not begin to keep up with inflation or even bank fees. Stung by previous declines, and bewildered by today's complexity and uncertainty, it's too easy for investors to imagine falling into a giant pothole if they take their foot off the brake.

Others, with a stiff upper lip, kept driving just as they did before. They stayed true to their investment discipline; and despite bone-jarring earthquakes (two of the worst bear markets in modern US history occurred within the first decade of this century), they stayed on the road, followed all the rules, and actually, as of this writing, are feeling somewhat vindicated, as the market did come back. Probe a little deeper, however, and you'll rarely find anyone who's confident that things have returned to normal. The widely used term *new normal* implies that the old rules about how to be a successful investor may no longer apply and that we need to fundamentally rethink our assumptions about economic growth. Even with the strong bounce of 2009–2014, overall stock market returns since the peak of 2000 are measly by historical standards: as of June 2014, real returns after inflation for the S&P 500 were just 1.2 percent annualized.[3]

This book is for both kinds of investors: the ones shivering in their parked cars, waiting for the fog to lift, and the ones on cruise control, telling themselves that everything is fine but unable to tune out the disturbing news that keeps intruding on the hour. Of course most of us can relate to each of them; some days we jump behind the wheel and crank up the tunes, just like the old days, but other times, perhaps after seeing too much carnage along the highway or hearing about an approaching storm, we hunker down and stay put.

Wherever you have been, our focus here is on helping you get where you want to go. To guide your way forward, this book offers a pairing of two central ideas: resiliency and embracing an expanded view of what it means to "invest."

The first, resiliency, offers an invaluable set of principles that can guide our decisions in this fast-changing world, keeping us responsive in the decades to come. The second arises from our experience as investment advisors, through which we have come to appreciate the pivotal role that investing plays in shaping the wholeness of our lives and our collective future.

By weaving together these two essential themes, we developed the framework that you are about to learn: resilient investing. This toolkit can help you build a life in accordance with your dreams, no matter what the future may bring. With it you'll learn how to take action, stand up to uncertainty, and stay flexible.

Here is a first peek at these two complementary ideas.

Resiliency

There's a new word in town, and its name is *resilience*. It came out of the blue and unseated the reigning champion, *sustainability*, which, as many had noted, was getting kind of soft (Barbie now comes in "sustainable packaging"). Everywhere we look resilience is poking in its fresh new face: in economics, climate science, leadership, online security, community planning, and psychology (actually that is a place where it's been in common usage for some time). Amazingly in these partisan times, it has managed to span the ideological spectrum. The Post Carbon Institute recently launched a companion website, while the World Economic Forum in Davos jumped on the bandwagon by focusing its 2013 conference on "Resilient Dynamism." If resilience science speaks simultaneously to relocalization activists in their transition towns, as well as the 1 percent gathered in their enclaves, we should clearly be paying attention!

Let's look at what is meant by resilience and why it has arisen from so many quarters as a concept that is truly emblematic of our times. Andrew Zolli's 2012 book, *Resilience: Why Things Bounce Back,* frames resilience as "the capacity of a system, enterprise, or a person to maintain its core purpose and integrity in the face of dramatically changed circumstances."[4] Zolli sees resilience as "an essential skill in an age of unforeseeable disruption and volatility." A unifying and powerful lens, resilience can focus our awareness and actions at all levels, for individuals, businesses, communities, nations, and the entire planet.

Many people become aware of the importance of resiliency only after a disaster. Do an online search for *Hurricane Sandy resiliency* and you will find numerous articles and conferences convened as decision makers tried to figure out what we could learn from this superstorm and how we might rebuild in ways that will leave people less vulnerable. But the time to focus on resilience is *before* disaster strikes; in 2014 President Barack Obama proposed a $1 billion "resiliency fund" to help communities protect themselves from climate change impacts such as floods, drought, and wildfires.[5]

Futurists and systems theorists are having a heyday, creating a menagerie of frameworks[6] describing resilience, but it really doesn't need to be a difficult concept—we see it all around us. Everyone over 40 knows that they are not as physically resilient as they used to be; injured children recover more quickly than injured grandparents. Healthy ecosystems bounce back from fires and storms better than degraded ecosystems. Technology companies become irrelevant if they fail to respond decisively when circumstances change: perhaps the most striking example is Kodak, once synonymous with the very idea of photography but left in the dust by the shift to digital imaging.

For those with a strong bent on ensuring that we maintain the viability of the biosphere, it is worth taking a moment to see why resilience is starting to displace sustainability as an organizing concept. Zolli points out that sustainability tries to come up with an "equilibrium point" in which a system stays in balance, but this is counter to how many natural and human systems operate. As architect and systems thinker William McDonough wryly asks, "Who simply wants a sustainable marriage?"[7] Resilience does rely on the principles of sustainability (unsustainable investments weaken the capacity of a system to maintain integrity), but it strives for a healthy dynamism rather than stasis.

The lens of resilience makes us more cognizant that for better or worse we have entered the age of the *Anthropocene*—a new term for a geological age in which humans have become the dominant factor shaping the world. Natural systems have been damaged to such a degree that we need to be prepared for random, extreme disruptions.[8] At the same time, resilience points out that we should be designing our systems, and our lives, so that we do more than survive such disruptions. We will want to "capture the upside," thriving and growing when exposed to volatility and disorder, while also seizing emerging new opportunities as they come into view.

For some, resilience has a flavor of hunkering down, waiting for disaster to hit, and coming out unscathed. That's not a very juicy way to live, and it is not what *we* mean by resiliency. Our goal as investors is to make things better, for ourselves and for the world. We are using *resiliency* in its most flexible and optimistic form, still loyal to the goals of sustainability (providing for the needs of the present without harming the future) and with eyes staying sharp for emerging prospects. Here is our new and improved definition:

> **Resilience helps us to thrive by:**
>
> - **anticipating and preparing for disturbance,**
>
> - **improving the capacity to withstand shocks,**
>
> - **rebuilding as necessary, and**
>
> - **adapting and evolving when possible.**

Resilience is a powerful remedy for our uncertain times. It helps us learn to live *with* the fundamental complexity of modern life. When the inevitable disruptions do hit the system, resilient investors will have the best possible shock absorbers to minimize being rattled and will be positioned to bounce back even better than before. Our favorite one-liner comes from Harvard business professor Rosabeth Moss Kanter, who wrote, "When surprises are the new normal, resilience is the new skill."[9]

An Expanded View of Investing

In our combined decades of work as investment advisors, we have had the privilege of sitting down and talking in depth with hundreds of clients about what matters most to them. One thing that kept coming up in these conversations is that, although they liked our "invest with your values" approach, they did not like thinking about investing very much. We, on the other hand, think that investing is really cool, a focal activity where people make decisions that change their lives and the world. Are we just geeks, or do we see something that others don't?

Eventually, we realized that most people have a rather narrow image in their minds about what "investing" really means. Do an image search on the word *investing,* and you will see lots of coins and dollar bills, graphs and charts, bullion bars and Wall Street suits. What generally comes to mind is that *investing is done by those who have extra money, to turn it into even more money, using the methods promoted by Wall Street.* While most of us are interested in becoming more prosperous, this concept of investing leaves many people out of the game; and even for those who do invest in this way, it is a cold and abstract prescription that fails to touch on what gives deeper meaning to our lives.

We say that it's time for a new approach. Rather than wrinkling up one's nose and doing "investing" the way we have been taught, we are asking people to take a step back and really think about what a powerful and creative role this activity could play in their lives. This begins with expanding our notion about what investing truly is, so try this on for size: *investing is something that we all do by directing our time, attention, energy, or money in ways that move us toward our future dreams, using a diverse range of strategies.*

Let's start with dismissing the popular notion that investing is an activity that is available only to those with discretionary capital to play with. The fact is, neither the investment nor the return must necessarily be in the form of money. Financial investments are just one side of the coin; on the flip side is time—our most precious resource. We can and should bring this to the investing table by being thoughtful about the ways we focus our attention and channel our energy. Throughout this book we look at ways that the choices you make with your time, attention, and energy are as central to your long-term investments as the ways you manage your money.

Next we rethink the purpose of investing. As the Beatles so joyously pointed out, money can't buy us love. Still, the single-minded pursuit of

most investors is to increase our financial "net worth," though our real
goals in life are much broader than that. Resilient investing recognizes
that we are actually interested in cultivating several types of assets:

- personal—relationships, community, learning, health, and
  spiritual growth;

- tangible—home, efficient energy systems, local food supplies,
  and a healthy local ecosystem; *and*

- financial—stocks, bonds, and savings.

By including all of these valued objectives in our resilient investment
plan, we have the opportunity to shape virtually all aspects of our lives.

Finally, it is important to rethink *how* we pursue those goals. Are
the recommendations proffered by traditional investment books, maga-
zines, and financial services firms the one and only valid methodology?
Are there other strategies that you can use to diversify and seek out new
opportunities that are largely ignored by Wall Street? And in this VUCA
world, might it be wise to consider the possibility that strict adherence to
traditional buy-and-hold-on-to-your-hats dogma may leave us vulnerable
to systemic risks that threaten to send our economy reeling?

We refer to this notion of spreading our wings into more spacious
skies as "weaning off Wall Street." It opens our minds to exploring strategies beyond the one that rules today's herd, with its all too familiar mantra
of "show me the money." As you are about to see, resilient investing
provides three novel approaches to mix and match: close to home, sustainable global economy, and evolutionary investing (see chapter 3).

Now, with our expanded resources (money *and* time) in hand, we
are pleased to show you our map. **SEE FIGURE 1** What you will see immediately is that it covers much more terrain than that old familiar basket
of market-based financial investments. There are nine distinct zones of
investment choices that form the Resilient Investing Map (RIM).

The north-south axis of the map reminds you to grow your personal
and tangible assets, not just your financial ones. Moving east to west, you

THREE CORE INVESTMENT STRATEGIES		
Close to Home	**Sustainable Global Economy**	**Evolutionary**
1 Family Nonprofit/faith Community health Personal resilience practices	**2** Values-based career Lifestyle choices Advocacy	**3** Inspiration and learning Embracing diversity (social, worldview, ecological) Personal/spiritual growth
4 Home/house/property Local infrastructure Energy systems/choices Local shopping and sharing	**5** Shopping with your values (products of the global economy)	**6** Regenerative investments (in physical world/nature) Ecosystem services Circular economy/ biomimicry Habitat conservation
7 Local investing (community banks, credit unions, loan funds, investment clubs)	**8** Sustainable and responsible investing (SRI mutual funds, stocks, bonds)	**9** Impact investing (in new systems and financial structures) Microfinance Crowdfunding

The left axis reads (bottom to top): THREE KINDS OF ASSETS / TYPES OF RETURN, with row labels **Personal/ Social**, **Tangible**, **Financial**.

Figure 1   *The Resilient Investing Map (RIM)*

will be engaging with three distinct investment strategies in ways that connect with both your interests and your outlook for the future.

You could think of each of the nine investment zones as baskets in which you can distribute the eggs (time and money) that you have to invest. By doing this you will achieve far more diversification than could be imagined from the limited perspective that most people are accustomed to using.

We will elaborate on this expanded approach to investing in chapters 1 through 4, and in chapters 5 through 8 we will guide you toward using the map to create your own resilient investing plan. Because this is a living landscape, we'll be fleshing out the map's many highways and byways, along with its connective rivers and verdant prairies, in a continually evolving online supplement to the book. In chapters 9 and 10, we'll share our own experiences of working with the Resilient Investing Map and envision a future in which each of the three strategies becomes widely adopted.

This book is an invitation to embark on a journey of exploration in service of a most concrete purpose: preparing your life for whatever may come. We will help you cultivate a deeper clarity about how to work toward your hopes and dreams for the future while accounting for the uncertainties inherent in looking beyond our visible horizons. The way forward is likely to be dangerous, exhilarating, and challenging; it can also be rewarding, nourishing, and joyful. We may not know which future awaits us around the bend—but the way there is clear: we'll just need to bend!

Future-Proofing Your Life

What are the advantages of adopting a map such as ours? Why would you want to be a "resilient" investor?

Many people are motivated by the desire to be as prepared as possible for an uncertain future, but they recognize that this is no easy task. We'll encourage you to take a big-picture view of the world and consider the many ways that the future could unfold. You will want to envision where you would like to be going both in the near term and in the years to come and to keep abreast of the wide and growing range of investment choices available. By thinking in this broad, creative way, resilient investing gives you the tools to design a personalized plan. This will show you where you are currently investing your time and money, highlight areas that you might be over- or underemphasizing, and provide the guidance you will need to move forward in your chosen directions.

As you put your plan into action, you will notice a *newfound sense of calm,* one that rests on the knowledge that you have taken measured steps to future-proof your life and are ready to ride out the inevitable storms and surprises that come your way. You cannot eliminate risk, but you can dial down your stress level and have more peace of mind from knowing that you are prepared. Having a *comprehensive and diverse set of investments* will provide genuine benefits when one or another market you have invested in has a downturn, whether it's a sudden drop in the Dow, a dry spell that decreases yields in your garden or regional food network, or an unexpected health challenge. While it is always painful to suffer a hit in one area, investments in other zones will likely be doing better and help carry you through.

We would be remiss if we didn't mention that this broader approach to investing, one that elevates goals such as fulfillment and meaning, can also bring *benefits to your financial bottom line.* Yes, making money and stewarding it well is very much part of the picture. Resilience focuses your selection of financial instruments toward ones that are most relevant to these times, and it brings new investment opportunities onto your radar. In your daily life, it can also serve you in more-fundamental ways; its big-picture lens helps you avert short-sighted mistakes, and it excels at pointing out ways to reduce expenses while increasing happiness.

Another key benefit of this framework is that it is designed to *keep you flexible and adaptable.* Part of the process is to regularly revisit and revise your plan. If there is an unforeseen event, resilient investors find a way to learn from the experience and emerge smarter and stronger. Think of a redwood tree: after a fire, it grows even sturdier and releases its seeds into the rich soil left behind. But even if disaster never strikes, resilient investing is smart investing. Its forward-looking approach helps you identify and seize new opportunities that others may miss.

Finally and perhaps most importantly, as you move through this book and take steps to boost your personal resiliency, you will also be *fostering resilience in our communities, our economy, and our environment.* The beauty of this approach is that the strategies that best prepare you and your family for a range of future scenarios are inherently beneficial to the systems upon which civilization and all life depend. Resilient investors strive to stay abreast of the changing world and participate in constructive ways, wherever it goes: to be part of the breakthroughs to a sustainable future, to prosper in a world that is muddling through, and to have foundations for sustenance and happiness in place if things start to crumble around us. While this resilient adaptability is central to effective personal decision making, it also enhances our collective ability to successfully traverse these times.

What makes this so groundbreaking is that you—the investor—need not base your decisions on any moral or ethical injunction to do the right thing. In many ways what we are proposing here can be seen as nothing more than a rational attempt to be prepared for multiple possible futures. Of course, we take it as a given that nearly everyone desires what is best for the world; it's this natural human tendency that in 1999 led us to call what we do "natural investing."[10] But we also know that many people make their investment choices, at least for financial assets, based strictly on their calculations of monetary risk and return. Resilient investing offers a big tent, one that welcomes anyone who wants to be proactive about their future.

For those who *are* motivated to intentionally weave personal values into their financial and life decisions, there are now many more ways than ever before to nudge the world forward: companies actively building an economy that thrives within the limits of our biosphere and the diversity of global cultures, community loan funds that foster opportunity and equality in societies worldwide, crowdfunding empowering innovation throughout the economy, and programs building local food systems and funding ecological regeneration. Your investment, banking, purchasing, and charitable choices can be part of any or all of this—and in so doing, you will be aligning your financial decisions with your desire to make the best of whatever is yet to come.

Meanwhile, the heart of the resilient investor's portfolio may well be in nonfinancial investments. We can all benefit from putting energy into our own well-being and personal growth. Your relationships, in family and community, will forever be the fertile soil from which your life grows. And the time and energy you invest in the place where you live will foster the tangible assets of the home, community, and ecosystem that you will be living in and relying on in the years to come. As you expand your investment horizons to include more than what you do with your money, you will stay connected with the *real* wealth in your life. And that is always your best investment!

CHAPTER 1

Facing the Future

Why We Are Expanding Your View of Investing

W E HAVE LAID OUT A RADICAL NEW MAP OF THE INVESTING universe, and we are inviting you to navigate your own path across this vast terrain. But before we start exploring the nooks and crannies, let's take a moment to ask the fundamental question: *why invest?*

Some would say this is obvious—we invest to build wealth. And what's the point of building wealth? To be secure? To then build even more security and more wealth? Isn't that what we all want? Well, no, at least not in the way it is usually presented. While we take it as a given that most people want to increase their financial assets (at least up to a point) and have some nice things, traditional measurements of personal wealth are inadequate, often ignoring that which gives us the most satisfaction. Economists measure our "standard of living," but what we are really after is a higher "quality of life"—and while there is overlap, those two are not the same thing! The point of investing, we would suggest, is not just about having more but about being happy in a full, classical sense.

Let's look back—back as far as 2,500 years—for help in answering these questions. Aristotle, writing in the *Nicomachean Ethics,* described the point of a well-lived life, the goal we should be aiming for, as "blessedness." For Aristotle blessedness meant enjoying family and friends, with a deep feeling of well-being and contentment. In our day this ideal might suggest a mature experience of knowing one's mission, succeeding at pursuing that mission, having a solid primary relationship and close friends and family, having sufficient financial resources to live well according to one's own standards, making a contribution and leaving a legacy one can be proud of, and staying in right relationship to the natural world that sustains life. It is not about *more*—it is about *better.*

We do not think of investing as simply a professional, numbers-crunching discipline; for us it is something much more fundamental. We believe investing should support financial goals (buy a house, start a business) *and* it should support the bigger and deeper and more profound purpose of a life—Aristotle's blessedness. Investing can help each of us live a better life, and it can help improve communities and build a better world for all.

To do this we must first break out of the confines that limit our ideas about wealth. Financial choices are just one part of a continual process of giving and receiving, balancing risk and reward, and exchanging time, energy, and money with those around you. So let's make room for values and communities, for society and the earth. And let's expand our vision to include the interior realms of emotional and spiritual well-being as well, which are enduring elements of healthy human development. By doing so we are bound to get results that are more relevant and more life-nourishing.

One World, Many Futures

Hopefully, you are feeling enticed to put some of your valuable time into this soaring vision of investing. Be aware, though: you're going to need a pioneering spirit. In these volatile, uncertain times, the old road maps that guided twentieth-century investors are obsolete. The landscape has changed, and you'll be traveling on new pathways that have yet to see much traffic. This can be disconcerting, as it lacks the appearance of stability—that Rock of Gibraltar that was once an icon of the financial industry but turned out to be a mirage.

The uncertainty that plagues today's investors became clear to us over the past several years, as clients and friends shared their notion that the world has come unmoored and that business-as-usual is no longer a reliable anchor for making decisions about their investments—or their lives. While these wide-ranging conversations are often rich with insight and full of passion, our role as investment advisors asks us to act from an objective view of the world, free of personal and emotional bias. As you can imagine, this is no easy task!

The global economy has proven to be remarkably resilient, having adapted and grown in spite of (or because of) dramatic, world-shaking events. So it seems likely that our fundamental social and economic structures will remain intact, at least into the near future. Yet the potential for disruption—sudden or slowly mounting social, economic, and environmental upheavals—has increased to the point that it may make sense to hedge our bets on that front.

On the other hand, we see that rapid advances in technology, along with the interconnection of global civil society, contain a wealth of creative promise that we have just barely begun to glimpse. This could catapult us forward more rapidly, and in different directions, than we have imagined.

With this awareness comes the need to give due consideration to several plausible futures that are beginning to emerge, co-existing in ways that are already visible. We will flesh these out more in chapter 6, but, for now, here is a sketch of the future landscapes that are coming into view. It's important to stress that we do not suggest that any one of these is likely to dominate our future or that they are equally likely—they are archetypal images that we'll be using in a much more nuanced way.

> ▶ **Global scenario 1: breakdown, "the long emergency"**
>   *Social, economic, and/or environmental meltdown,*
>   *leaving the global economy in tatters*

> ▶ **Global scenario 2: muddle through down, "relentless struggle"**
>   *Rolling recessions amid a failure to address the systemic*
>   *causes of social, economic, and environmental decline*

▶ **Global scenario 3: muddle through up, "incremental progress"**
Gradual improvement of key quality-of-life indicators within the status quo framework of political and economic systems

▶ **Global scenario 4: breakthrough, "rational emergence"**
Exponential social innovation, new technologies, and the evolution of wisdom/consciousness to deploy them wisely

What do you think? Are there any that seem absolutely impossible to you? Can you imagine that aspects of any and all of these descriptions could come to fruition?

Most people have been making investment and life plans based on the assumption that we will continue living under some variation of a muddle-through scenario. Relatively few have seriously considered, let alone prepared for, scenarios that upend the status quo structures upon which these investments rely. Of those who have taken action, some have done so in a reactive way, rashly bailing out from the global economy in anticipation of some sort of apocalypse, or perhaps dreaming of a prophetic worldwide awakening.

But preparing for a range of possibilities can be done in a healthy and balanced way. As a resilient investor, you'll want to at least consider them all and will likely take some steps that will help you adapt to any scenario you see as possible, even the ones that you consider unlikely. This will help you face the future with fresh eyes and provides a framework that lets you move forward with confidence.

Time for More Baskets!

Diversification is, at its root, a response to the ancient admonition you might have learned from Grandma: don't put all of your eggs in one basket. If that basket drops, they could all break, ruining your and Grandma's breakfast! This proverb can be traced back to the seventeenth century and was popularized by Cervantes in *Don Quixote*.[1] (Later, Mark

Twain, ever the contrarian, proposed the exact opposite: "Put all your eggs in the one basket and—*watch that basket!*"[2])

The wisdom of Cervantes goes nearly unquestioned today. Virtually every reputable financial firm teaches people about diversification, extolling the importance of spreading out risk. But—and this is an important *but*—we contend that however well intentioned, Wall Street's version suffers from two major omissions: first, Wall Streeters focus solely on one's financial instruments; second, they cannot model the possibilities of breakdown/breakthrough, so they presume that we will muddle through for the foreseeable future.

These blind spots have led investors to focus nearly all of their attention on investments made within a single zone on the RIM (zone 8: financial assets/global economy). A good financial advisor will ensure that you are diversified *within* that basket[3] and might even offer advice on real estate (zone 4: tangible assets/close to home), but this is far different from being offered enough baskets to fill the RIM. A more accurate metaphor is a bunch of small dividers (subcategories of types of stocks and bonds) placed within the basket that contains Wall Street's financial instruments.

So instead of following Grandma's wise advice, people are unwittingly using Mark Twain's approach, one that was meant to be a parody! We are putting everything into one large basket, hoping and praying that we don't trip and that nothing bad happens to the global economy, either of which could send our eggs tumbling. This may sound humorous, but it leaves people far more vulnerable than they have been led to believe.

Resilient investing takes the virtue of well-considered asset allocation and applies it to a wider set of holdings. Obviously, there is so much that will not fit in Twain's single container, including all of your personal assets and most of your tangible ones—the very investments that will serve to buoy you through the ups and downs of your financial holdings. We are making the case for creating a truly balanced portfolio that includes much more than you will ever find on a brokerage statement.

And what happens if the future is not simply an extrapolation of muddling through? Wall Street's methods have worked well during many market cycles, but they offer scant protection from systemic risk—the risk of collapse of the overall market, not just a particular company or industry. In financial-speak, another word for *systemic risk* is *undiversifiable risk*,[4] which essentially says that there is nothing in the global economy basket that will keep you afloat when the ship goes down.

The recent financial crisis provided a glimpse of what this could look like. Real estate values collapsed, uprooting homeowners who had been lulled into a fantasy world where prices only go up. Bond prices gyrated, as the risk of default by corporations and municipalities rose, causing great distress among older investors who thought they were invested conservatively. Even gold, regarded as a safe haven by many, sank 25 percent during the worst of the 2008 crisis.[5] Investors had no place to hide except under the mattress.

Nobody knows when the next shock will hit the financial system, but if there was one lesson to learn, it was that investors need to update their risk management toolbox. We are not willing to accept that there is no way to address systemic risks, and neither should you. A resilient investing plan will enrich your life in today's world while hedging against—or, if you choose, preparing for—the possibility that our fundamental social, economic, and environmental reality could shift in profound ways. Of course, while resilient investing may reduce exposure to systemic risk, we also must remain diligent and conscious of managing (and balancing) the range of specific risks inherent in our actions across the RIM; this is addressed in brief in Resource 2: The Investor's Eye (at the back of the book) and in more detail on ResilientInvestor.com.

Our nine different baskets offer a much wider array of places to entrust your investments. Remember that baskets are one of humanity's oldest inventions—practical, sturdy, beautiful, even (dare we say) resilient containers—and have been put to myriad uses through the ages. As you make your way through the next three chapters, you are bound to realize that you have already been putting some eggs into many of these resilient investing baskets but lacked a framework for seeing how they fit into your overall picture. The RIM helps us be mindful about all of our investments—including those made with our time and attention.

Diversification may not be an elegant term, but it comes from *diversify*, which means to expand and broaden our horizons. Now it's time to do exactly that, as we escape from the box that limits most investors to mainstream financial offerings. Let's unfold the Resilient Investing Map and set off on our journey of discovery!

CHAPTER 2

More Than Money: Recognizing Your *Real* Net Worth

Personal, Tangible, and Financial Assets

THE RESILIENT INVESTING MAP INVITES YOU TO INVEST IN YOUR LIFE in a way that recognizes and grows *all* of your assets. Indeed the goal of resilient investing is to consciously and methodically spread your time and money around the full RIM to nourish all the elements of your *complete* "net worth." This will include prudence with your money (financial assets), appreciation of your possessions and the built and natural world (tangible assets), and nourishing your relationships and inner growth (personal assets). **SEE FIGURE 2**

It may feel a little strange to think of, say, the ways you prioritize activities that enhance your child's well-being *and* the strategies you are using to manage a brokerage account as being parts of a unified investment system. We're trained to think of these as very different kinds of decisions, but they are indeed related, as both are investments you make to bring about a desired result in the future.

Resilient investing enables you to put all of your goals on the table as you consider where you want to direct your time, attention, and money. Crucially, this approach acknowledges that for most people financial resources are limited. Those who cannot set aside money to invest should

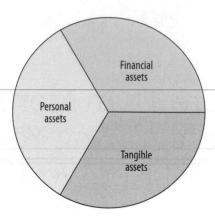

Figure 2   *Your Real Net Worth*

realize that they are indeed making investment decisions that are just as important—maybe more so—than those who are fortunate enough to have a brokerage account. At the same time, by looking beyond financial investments, we encourage *everyone* to diversify their investment horizons to include the equally important tangible and personal realms. The ways you engage and are nourished by your home and your ecosystem, and the crucial roles of your loved ones and the pursuit of your dreams, are at least as important as your portfolio balance.

Let's take a closer look at your *real* net worth by taking a ramble along the rows of the RIM.

Financial Assets

Financial assets, the bottom row of the RIM, are the familiar currency of the realm that we are used to calling "investments." This may include corporate stocks, debt instruments (i.e., bonds) that loan money to governments or corporations, and your short-term savings and checking accounts. Mutual funds, and now exchange-traded funds (ETFs), were created to help ordinary investors diversify their holdings of stocks and bonds. Wall Street also offers more complex instruments, ranging from relatively simple options contracts to a bewildering array of derivatives and bundled risk instruments that most of us, professionals included, would be stretched to comprehend (which is how their creators like it!). Those who have substantial assets or higher incomes may access the world of private investments and hedge funds.

For those who seek a "triple bottom line" (social, environmental, *and* financial), it has long been possible to select financial assets that align with one's personal values.[1] Most of the above choices are available through sustainable and responsible investing (SRI), and performance has been reliably competitive (see Resource 1: The Case for SRI). In recent years community investing has created many opportunities to bank locally as well as to put some savings into community loan funds that do great work. Opportunities to participate in microfinance in the developing world or to loan your money to programs supporting local food systems are increasing every year, while qualified investors can choose among a wide range of private placement offerings in social enterprises that serve sectors such as education, healthcare, renewable energy, green development, and sustainable agriculture and forestry.

Crowdfunding is one of the newest innovations, enabling people to directly support startup companies and arts, social change, or environmental projects; though not fully implemented as of this writing, legislation passed in 2012 is designed to allow small investors (as opposed to high-net-worth investors, who already have this right) to make modest investments in companies that are just getting started or that wish to expand. It holds great promise for individuals who wish to invest locally and for small businesses that can now access the capital markets.

Tangible Assets

Tangible assets are the "stuff" that we own or have access to; these occupy the middle row of the RIM. Most important are the practical aspects of daily life on which our survival and happiness depend: food, water, clothing, energy, land, buildings, transportation, and technology. Whenever we trade our time, energy, or money for anything physical—whether we hold it personally, like a well-forged shovel, or collectively, like a shared summer cabin—it becomes one of our tangible assets. It is easy to overlook this realm when thinking of our investments, especially those that are not "liquid," or readily resold.

Our decisions about which and how many tangible assets to invest in are often at the center of our economic lives and practice of investing. We are constantly faced with choices about when to convert some of our financial assets into tangible assets. While our homes and property are commonly considered "investments" because of their potential to gain value, this is the exception rather than the rule among tangible assets, many of which degrade in resale value quite quickly. We often choose to buy something that we know will never provide a financial payback because we believe it will enrich our lives in other ways. In addition, our possessions make apparent the impact we have on the world through our purchasing choices—all that stuff we have in our houses and garages offers the opportunity to contemplate the natural and human resources that were required to make and transport it to us.

But tangible assets also extend beyond the things within our personal grasp. The burgeoning "sharing economy" surely involves tangible assets, whether it's owning tools collectively with others or joining a car-sharing service that provides you with a vehicle when you need it. You might choose to invest in local food security by joining a community-supported agriculture (CSA) farm.[2] The parks, libraries, and other shared resources we enjoy in our communities are also part of our tangible portfolio.[3] On a larger scale, you may decide to support efforts that create tangible benefits to the local or global community and the biosphere. This could include things like habitat conservation and wildlife corridor projects around the globe, efforts to keep water rights with the land rather than sold to distant cities, and investments that conserve agricultural land for future generations of farmers. Ultimately, a healthy, functioning ecosystem is our most fundamental tangible asset, one that we all hold in common.

Personal and Social Assets

Personal and social assets (which we refer to simply as personal assets) compose the row that we are least likely to think of as part of our investment choices, and for that reason we'll invest a few more words in this section! Though it's off our investment radar, this is humanity's oldest asset class and is still the one in which many of us are most actively engaged. Here we take care of ourselves—mind, heart, body, and soul—as well as nurture the web of social relationships that define us: partner, family, neighborhood, school, church, community, culture, country, and even global social networks.

Our social, interpersonal relationships are an essential kind of wealth that cannot be ignored; they require dedicated investment to reap the human returns that we each need in our life. We all have many examples in our personal lives of the ways that friends, family, and professional, recreational, or faith networks have carried us through our times of greatest need. In the face of the complexity and uncertainty that we are addressing throughout this book, these personal assets are likely to be the most stable and valuable form of investment that most of us hold. Best of all, they tend to reap the highest returns when times are rough.

Volunteering at a local soup kitchen, joining advocacy groups and getting active in politics, and pitching in at your kid's school—all are ways to invest and grow your personal assets. It is widely accepted that altruistic and charitable actions not only help the intended recipient but also give the donor substantial benefits ranging from stress reduction to being held in higher esteem in the community.[4]

Lifestyle choices can build these assets, as well. This might be simple things like working in your garden or learning to do your own plumbing repair, activities that build your personal assets (enjoyment and skills) while adding to your tangible assets (nicer home) and conserving financial assets. How do you want to invest your leisure time? Does a little voice in your head whisper that it's time to make a career change? One corollary of complexity is that we now have many more choices, over more aspects of life, than any generation that came before us. This means we have more decisions to make, but it also provides us with more opportunities to shape our lives in very personal ways.

The same is true for your family; giving generously of your time, money, and attention to encourage their interests and growth will have a positive impact on your life as well as theirs. Sharing music and the arts, exploring and learning about nature by hiking and camping together, supporting their education and personal development—all will show rich returns in your relationships and in the lives of your kids as they come of age. For those with the means, taking even one trip abroad to show American children what life is like for people in other countries is a powerful reality check that can foster a feeling of gratitude and appreciation for their own lives as well as a social consciousness that can guide them toward ethical choices.

And then there's the *really* personal: taking care of yourself. Here are your most internal investments: diet and exercise choices that foster health, education, and lifelong learning in a range of forms as well as spiritual nourishment and growth. Sometimes taking a walk is all you need to regain some perspective; at those times that walk is the best investment you can make. Other times you might really need to buckle down and learn some new skills, or dedicate time to healing a chronic condition.

Again, these are the kinds of investment decisions we make all the time, but by being mindful of the choices we're making we can become more aware of how they support, or do not support, the goals we're pursuing with our other assets.

Putting energy into your community, improving your relationship skills, participating in both real-world and online networks relevant to your interests—all are ways to strengthen the personal and social elements of a resilient life. When you invest time and money in things you believe in, the intangible returns that flow back can often outshine the financial returns that are overemphasized in our society. Forming and growing these connections builds your *social capital,* a value term that even economists can appreciate.

Finally, many people find essential meaning by cultivating their spiritual life. One of the bounties of living in these times is our access to a wide range of wisdom traditions sourced from many cultures and eras. Organized religion falls into this realm, as do both secular and nonsecular meditative practices. Or perhaps you prefer engagement with nature as a restorative and balancing force. There are many paths, but by acknowledging and connecting to a greater whole within which one's own life plays out, and learning to quiet the chatter of our minds, we can find ourselves gaining in both purpose and direction.

In fact, many of the authors who have been thinking about this age of complexity are strong advocates of investing time and energy into one's spiritual life, citing returns that include cultivating a grounded sense of equanimity and calmness as well as the development of capacities for insight and integration, essential qualities that will always be there for us as we head into the unknowable future.

It is appropriate that this forms the top row of our map, as many of us tend to downplay the importance of nurturing what integral theory philosopher Ken Wilber terms our "interiors."[5] By embracing personal assets as something you actually *invest* in, resilient investing has embedded within itself the practice of considering these essential realms whenever we make important decisions about our future.

CHAPTER 3

Weaning off Wall Street

The Three Investment Strategies:
Close to Home, Sustainable Global Economy,
and Evolutionary

As we turn our focus toward the columns of the Resilient Investing Map, it is time to recall our quick survey of the VUCA world—volatile, uncertain, complex, and ambiguous—in which we live. There's an unfathomable intertwining of relationships that underlies the global economy and the physical world, making predictions virtually impossible. As financial advisors it has not been easy for us to overcome our desire for certainty about where the world is heading. But once we acknowledged that the world as it is may not be sitting on the most solid of foundations—and that our clients hold a range of views about our possible futures—it became essential to explore strategies that speak to both emerging innovations and local resilience.

Even a few years ago, such a multifaceted approach would have been impractical, as there were few opportunities to invest our money in either the close-to-home or evolutionary strategy. Now we are energized by the explosion of creativity taking place in virtually all the RIM zones—particularly for one's financial assets, where it is increasingly possible to select options that do not come from Wall Street. In recent years formerly obscure niches, such as international microfinance, local food systems, and "social purpose bonds," have catapulted into categories recognized by institutional investors. The World Economic Forum describes these outside-the-box approaches as moving "from the margins to the mainstream."[1] And while some of the ways to invest in personal and tangible assets are timeless, here too there have been exciting innovations, many of which—such as the sharing economy—have been empowered by technological advances.

In this chapter we look at how each of the strategies has a unique mindset, one derived from, but not locked to, the scenarios we explored earlier. In chapter 4 we flesh out the nine zones with a few examples so you can get a taste for how each strategy suggests different ways that you can grow your personal, tangible, and financial assets.

STRATEGY 1

Investing Close to Home: Strengthening Our Foundations

Home is where the heart is. And the hearth, and the art, and where the health of the whole earth is tended. *Eco,* the root of the words *economics* and *ecology,* comes from *oikos,* the Greek word for "home." The close-to-home strategy brings economics back to its roots, to the household, community, and systems that support our most fundamental well-being. Close-to-home investing recognizes that much of what we already spend time, money, and attention on are rightly considered investments. Our personal health and skills, family and home, community organizations, and intimate, professional, and community relationships—all are addressed in this strategy. (Today many of us have nourishing family and community ties both where we live and in other places as well; these more distant relationships may be part of your close-to-home strategy, though we focus on the local in this narrative.)

If this strategy seems familiar, it may be because it's in our bones, as this is what all investing was for most of human history. Although it is common in the modern age to not even consider investing in one's hometown, in the past this was the *only* place that most people spent, loaned, and invested their money; even our time at work was usually at a local business rather than as part of the global economy. Now, as then, the lion's share of our time (at least away from work) is spent close to home, and a big chunk of investment wealth may be here, as well: our literal home—a house and land—is the largest (and often only) asset many people own.

Beyond this, remember that we all begin close to home. When you are young and just starting out—or if you are recovering from a setback or don't have many financial resources—focusing your attention here is likely your best strategy. By *close to home* in this context, we mean *very* close! We think of Warren Buffett's comment: "Investing in yourself is the best thing you can do....If you have true talent yourself, and you have maximized your talent, you have a terrific asset."[2] Invest in yourself, in your knowledge and skills; use your time and focus your attention toward improving your own ability to create value for other people. Because the return from such activities can be significant, this personal initiative can be your biggest source of wealth—and it is almost always your first.

A simple guideline for the close-to-home strategy is to invest in what you know, in what you can see and touch, and in who and what is around you. As famed Fidelity investor Peter Lynch liked to say, "Never invest in any idea you can't illustrate with a crayon." (We imagine close-to-home Lynch pointing to a child's drawing of a house with a big apple tree, a smiling neighbor, and yellow sun rays reaching down to some solar panels.) Local investments that are close at hand are easier to track and influence; when you are close to what you are invested in, you can intervene if there is a problem and weigh in on positive change. Try that with a mutual fund!

Close-to-home investing is fundamentally about relationships, asking us to enter into more intimate, face-to-face engagements. Returning more of our focus to this time-tested strategy represents a rebalancing as we step back from our immersion in a global system, which Don Shaffer of RSF Social Finance describes as "complex, opaque, and anonymous, based on short-term outcomes,"[3] and we begin to embrace the virtues of local engagement, which is "more direct, transparent, and personal, based on long-term relationships."[4] Shopping at the farmers market, you exchange cash for carrots. You can see exactly how orange and crisp they are and talk with the farmer who grew them—if the carrots are sweet, you'll be back for more. The close-to-home strategy seeks to apply the same immediacy and connection to its other investment activities.

In *Local Dollars, Local Sense,* a thorough survey of the local investment movement, Michael Shuman makes a compelling case that small businesses constitute about half the gross domestic product (GDP) of the United States, but most investors are completely missing out.[5] Over-investing in Wall Street and underinvesting in Main Street (and other close-to-home strategies) is a diversification problem that this book, and especially this strategy, intends to help you overcome. As mentioned earlier, while this type of financial investment has been difficult at best for most of us, there are encouraging developments under way.

While everyone is involved with at least some, and usually many, close-to-home activities, there are two groups for whom this has become the main focus of their resilient investing practice. The first works to enliven local economies, primarily because of the positive effects that enhanced community resilience would offer in any possible future, and secondarily as a hedge against systemic economic shocks. They bank local, buy local, and invest in local businesses. Transition Towns and many other local and regional initiatives[6] are engaged in such proactive "going local" efforts.

Others choose investments close to home to prepare for systemic breakdown, with an emphasis on personal and family survival, and in some cases to strengthen regional resilience.[7] Their goal is to increase their odds of surviving "the end of the world as we know it."[8] Some are "preppers," caching food, water, and ammunition on the edge of civilization, while others are deep ecologists who believe we have passed irreversible ecological tipping points and that their energy is best used in personal and regional preparedness.

We might playfully label folks from these two perspectives "bloomers" and "doomers." For the bloomers, with the intention of building community resilience, the paramount goals are diverse local ownership, sustainability, and helping "dollars stay in the local economy to improve quality of life for all."[9] Doomers, who aim to ride out "the big reset"[10] through personal resilience, see self-sufficiency and protection against threats as primary; some also stress moral integrity and charity.[11] Both perspectives put a premium on good soil, heirloom skills, personal health, and freedom from dependency. The close-to-home strategy includes both of these camps and more, including small actions taken as modest hedges against the possibility of systemic shocks and all the ways that engagement in community fosters cherished human values. As long-standing community activists, we are motivated more by the desire to be proactive, but we also resonate with the wisdom of being prepared.

True to its name, the close-to-home strategy shines brightest when we make investment decisions about our home itself: choosing a region, community, and specific location we feel good about and making our home and yard a reflection of who we are.

One example of how deeply engaging this process can be is permaculture, a form of ecological design that integrates a host of close-to-home strategies, including home-scale gardening and agroforestry, renewable energy systems, community planning, and much, much more. A marriage of the old and the new, permaculture systems are a tangible expression of the close-to-home investing impulse. As permaculture co-founder David Holmgren reminds us, "In pre-industrial society, the nonmonetary economies of the household and community, based on love, reciprocity, gift and barter, were the bulk of the economy."[12] Regardless of what camp you might be in or how the future plays out, who wouldn't like more love, reciprocity, and gifts in their life?

STRATEGY 2

Sustainable Global Economy Investing: Raising the Bar

As exciting as it may be to expand your notions of investing to include the full range of strategies we describe here, much of the resilient investor's focus is likely to remain in the familiar realm of the existing global economy. That is where most of us have sought to build our financial assets (via salary and investment gains), and it is where we purchase most of our tangible assets: our transportation (whether personal or public, via airplanes or kayaks), our nifty gadgets (from juicers to smartphones), our food, our clothes—the list really does go on and on. Few of us would opt to give this up; we actively enjoy the fruits of this consumer cornucopia, many of which enrich our lives and empower our work and social engagement in profound ways. The role of this investment strategy is to help you work *within* the existing system as effectively as possible, making wise decisions and sound investments that move you toward your life goals.

Our approach to engaging with the global economy is, as the strategy's name suggests, oriented toward nudging it into higher standards of environmental ethics and social justice—two key elements of sustainability *and* resiliency. We are asking more from all the players—governments, corporations, and individuals—because our world *needs* us to do more. By making sustainable choices as we engage with the global economy as citizens, consumers, and investors, our actions within the global economy will be aligned with our activities in the other two strategies.

But do not let our talk of ethics and standards mislead you—the quintessential goal of making money remains central here. Successful engagement with the global economy provides a billowing tailwind that helps us sail into a more abundant future. As we grow our financial assets, we may choose to convert a portion of them into tangible and personal assets, and we can save for major expenses: retirement, house purchase, kids' college education, vacations, charitable giving, and the like. And while we agree with the critiques of equating GDP growth with societal well-being,[13] it is also clear that the surplus generated by a thriving economy *could* be harnessed to reduce poverty and address environmental concerns.

Just as with the other two strategies, there is lots of room for making personal choices that reflect your own particular areas of interest. Some of you may be adamant about reshaping the corporate structures and priorities that underlie today's global economy. Or you might diligently consider the climate, habitat, or social impact of your purchasing decisions. Others will focus on investing in particular green sectors (such as renewable energy, natural foods, and worker-owned businesses), or will prioritize building a career that expresses their values. While a full-on sustainability warrior may do all of this, most of us are likely to pick a few fronts on which to add our two cents to the direction of the global economy.

This strategy is rooted in the muddle-through-up scenario, one in which the world moves toward a more prosperous future. Herein lies one of the trickiest realms for the resilient investor to navigate: our efforts to achieve sustainability (so that we can muddle through *up*) are taking place within a market-driven economy, one that entices us with "low prices" but does not account for social and environmental costs (and so pulls us toward muddle through *down*). Every time we buy gas for our car, patronize a chain store, or go out to eat, we are straddling the line between our ideals and what is readily available today. Buy your shoes at a locally owned shoe store: the shoes still came from somewhere, and it was probably not a local cobbler; that smartphone you rely on could be filled with the spoils of remote mining activity and oppressive working conditions. And even when there is a greener choice, it may cost more, so you might not be able to afford it!

Indeed our sustainable global economy strategy coexists uneasily with the status quo global economy; suffice it to say, you will find lots of opportunities for honesty and self-reflection as your well-intentioned actions leave you short of where you would like to be. Often you'll have to settle for taking incremental steps. The best advice we know of to resolve these sorts of quandaries comes from a line in a Jiminy Cricket song, the one where he teaches Pinocchio how to make tough decisions, which is to "always let your conscience be your guide."[14]

Perhaps the most significant personal-level engagement we have with the global economy is our career choice. To what degree are you able to make a living while also gaining inner satisfaction from this huge investment of your time and attention? What aspects of your resilient life goals can you bring to bear in your work and with your work colleagues? How do you strike a balance between the demands of earning money and all of your other interests? Asking questions like these taps our desire to play a meaningful role in people's lives and to participate in the creation of a better world.

This same sense of personal connection can come into play while making financial investment decisions, a realm that has traditionally omitted this sort of reflection. Once we recognize that we have some leverage as stock owners, we can use it to effect positive change within the companies we invest in or to urge more-responsible corporate practices within the system as a whole. This has become somewhat easier to do as more corporations issue disclosure reports about their environmental, social, and governance (ESG) practices.

One result of our instant access to information is that we are increasingly aware of the consequences of our actions—and our inactions. This can lead people to decide *not* to invest in—or to boycott—the products of certain companies or even entire industries.

When garment factories in Bangladesh catch on fire or collapse, we learn which clothing brands ultimately bear responsibility for those deadly, inhumane working conditions.[15] Exploding oil wells and the relentless progression of extreme weather events has led to calls for institutions to divest from fossil fuel companies[16] and to the creation of a new category of sustainable mutual funds that are fossil fuel–free.[17] And when the big banks' risky and unethical practices caused a systemic financial meltdown, erasing a decade of market gains and putting millions of people out of work or their homes, the notion of "too big to fail" led to the "Move Your Money" campaign[18] that helped people switch to local and regional banks so that their savings would support communities rather than foster reckless speculation.

The global economy has clearly produced remarkable social progress, but today there is a sense that things are stagnating, as if the economy is suffering from chronic fatigue syndrome. From 2003 to 2013, the inflation-adjusted net worth of the median household in the United States fell 36 percent.[19] There is widespread doubt about whether the youth of today will have lives that are as good as their parents'. Concern about income inequality has soared as we watch the rich get richer while the middle class stagnates and the poor suffer the brunt of every downturn. And although the environment usually does not rank as high in polls when compared with these pocketbook issues, science is telling us that we really ought to be alarmed.

Many citizens are eagerly looking for strategies—both political and economic—to address these threatening storm clouds. The sustainable global economy strategy offers just that. It is based on the premise that our economic system can be changed from within, making it less exploitative and better able to meet human needs. Business-as-usual has a lot of momentum, so it's not going to reorient itself overnight; moreover these sorts of changes will not happen without effort. They require an engaged populace, working with persistence and using every possible leverage point to nudge the global economy toward a brighter future. Fortunately, there is plenty that you can do right now.

STRATEGY 3

Evolutionary Investing: Transformative Solutions

Evolution. The word conjures up images of strange creatures on the Galapagos Islands or perhaps of fundamentalists in Kansas trying to ban the study of Darwin's ideas. But our choice of this word to describe our most visionary strategy transcends biology. In *Evolutionaries: Unlocking the Spiritual and Cultural Potential of Science's Greatest Idea,* Carter Phipps defines *evolution* as "a broad set of principles and patterns that generate novelty, change, and development over time."[20] Since the nineteenth century, practitioners from many fields of study have found that an evolutionary framework helps explain the directional trajectory of knowledge—and that direction is ever forward!

Evolutionary investors are fueled by a conviction that "the principles of evolution are at work in our world today, helping to shape a future that will be better than the past."[21] The irrepressible human urge to experiment, make progress, and, yes, evolve is as strong today as it was in the twentieth century, a time when many science-fiction dreams became reality. At this very moment, people are working on breakthrough innovations that could address our most intractable problems: poverty, energy, the state of our planet, how to make our governments function better—in short, how we can live happy, fulfilled lives within a stronger, more resilient civilization.

Putting at least a slice of our pie into evolutionary directions is, in part, simply a wise, forward-looking approach to investing. It prepares us to take advantage of opportunities that others might miss, and it positions us to prosper in a world where humanity's higher aspirations begin manifesting. Today's most visionary investors are looking for exponential breakthroughs that may take a decade or more to come to fruition.

But let's not pretend that the only reason to invest with an evolutionary eye is self-interest. Its brightest allure is that it offers us ways to *actively participate* in the progression of culture, science, politics, economics, and, perhaps most challenging, ourselves. Here we can satisfy our yearning to create a legacy for future generations, to "place our own hands on the levers of [evolutionary] processes and make a positive impact."[22] Thanks to the access that we now have to information, and to crowdfunding tools like Kickstarter, we can learn about and fund projects that spark our imagination; likewise, online collaborations are opening ever more opportunities to design our own livelihoods.

This strategy goes well beyond the sustainable global economy strategy, in which we focus on ways to incrementally improve the effectiveness of today's existing structures. With evolutionary investing, we are working with a fresh palette. The invitation is to create a new vision of the world we wish to see, and then to invest our time or money into creating that world. David Korten calls for "a deep cultural and institutional transformation grounded in a story of unrealized human possibility."[23] Charles Eisenstein guides his audience to reach for "the more beautiful world our heart tells us is possible."[24]

Be alert for the little synchronicities of life that might be showing you the way. Perhaps you will meet someone whose wisdom and insight stop you in your tracks. Maybe it's an article you read or someone who touches you directly with their inspired actions. By having your evolutionary antenna up, you'll be ready for those moments.

This does not mean leaving pragmatism out of the picture, but it does ask us to stretch into our most imaginative and innovative selves. Remember, what may seem impractical right now may prove to be viable, and profitable, if it truly meets the needs of our times. Who would have thought that we would see someone like Elon Musk set two companies—a car manufacturer and a solar installer—on a disruptive course aimed at enabling people not only to avoid gas stations but also to unplug from the electric grid?[25] Or that two young design graduates would found Airbnb, which now books more rooms than most hotel chains? Less well known but perhaps even more remarkable is the leaderless, bottom-up emergence of over a million organizations working to advance human society, as documented by Paul Hawken in *Blessed Unrest*.

Broadly speaking, there are two major tributaries feeding the evolutionary river, and both are swelling with fresh ideas. The evolutionaries riding these currents are engaged in the core activities of this strategy: the redesign of existing social and technological systems and the creation of brand-new ones.

On one stream you will find the "new economy advocates." Paddling hard through treacherous rapids, these pioneers sense that the only way we'll achieve long-term, shared prosperity is by making structural changes to the economic system. People like Marjorie Kelly of the Tellus Institute,

Hazel Henderson of Ethical Markets, Gar Alperovitz of the New Economy Coalition, and John Fullerton of Capital Institute, to name a few, point out that the current system skews toward those who control vast amounts of the world's wealth and, if left unchecked, will take us over a waterfall. They cite real-life initiatives aimed at meeting human needs and creating the conditions that will allow life to thrive for generations to come.[26]

Sailing along the second branch is a flotilla of elegant, traditional craft and futuristic vessels. They are ferrying the planet's "research and development team" into uncharted territory, tackling the dysfunctions of government, education, healthcare, and virtually all the systems on which we depend. Running this stretch of river can provide some real thrills! Finding it can be as simple as following a new tech site[27] or viewing a TED talk, which can open your mind to ideas and innovations that you never imagined. Perhaps you will catch someone like Amory Lovins, who for decades has been reinventing our energy and transportation systems, showing us how to wean off oil and coal and revitalize our economy.[28] Or Peter Diamandis, who says that "abundance for all is within our grasp" and maps out plausible steps to get there.[29] But today's leaders are following in some big footsteps. Buckminster Fuller's books and inventions have inspired generations of innovators. He summed up the evolutionary mindset in this way: "You never change things by fighting the existing reality; [instead] build a new model that makes the existing model obsolete."[30]

At the confluence of these branches is the capacity for inward reflection, the ability to view not only the outer world but also our interior qualities as a system that is capable of evolving. Albert Einstein, who would certainly qualify as an evolutionary, said it best: "We can't solve problems by using the same kind of thinking that we used when we created them." People who embrace this path take time to unplug from daily distractions so that they can consider a bigger perspective, have the courage to see their own strengths and weaknesses, invest some time into practices that can help them grow, and, last but not least, take action. It is all well and good to learn about cutting-edge projects, but when you come across something that compels you, it's time to stop naval gazing, grab your paddle, and get into the flow. (Extra credit if you caught that pun!)

As we have emphasized throughout, this strategy does not depend on having the world move decisively toward its related breakthrough scenario. If muddling through remains the dominant scenario, or if we slip into a version of breakdown, you may still reap tremendous value by allocating a portion of your resources using this strategy. Just as, for example, there have been many successful investments in renewable energy, even while the energy system is dominated by fossil fuels, there is plenty of room for innovative, effective ideas to flourish within less-than-ideal circumstances. And as we will see, investments of your personal and tangible assets using this strategy make sense regardless of how things unfold in the near future.

In the investment world, the earliest investors in startups are known as "angel investors"; they are willing to take a chance on someone's new idea because they believe in the person and want to help the innovation succeed. Evolutionary investing is where each of us, to subsume a term that is generally reserved for wealthy investors, can become angel investors for the future, helping foster novelty, change, and development. We hope you see this as a delightful prospect! But it's also our duty to remind you that investments using this strategy often entail a high degree of risk. Whether you are personally trying new things or investing in people doing something that has not been tried before, you will want to keep your feet on the ground even as you aim for the stars.

The Missing Fourth Strategy: Show Me the Money!

As we have built the framework for the RIM, you may have noticed that we laid out four future scenarios in chapter 1 but are offering only three investment strategies. What's up with that?

There is indeed a strategy that meshes with a muddle-through-down scenario, one that is as familiar to us as water is to fish. But just as a fish might not realize that it's surrounded by water, we seldom notice just how immersed we are in business as usual. With this approach, which we call show me the money, we do three things:

- Position ourselves to "get ahead" in the job world

- Seek to find a "good deal" when we go shopping

- Select investments using solely financial metrics

Show me the money offers easy-to-understand guidance on how to allocate our personal, tangible, and financial assets. It comes across as a good and proper way to live in the modern world, so much so that it is hard to think of it as a strategy per se. It actually functions more as a subconscious default response; we rarely stop to consider that it is just one possible choice among many. Our purpose in shining a light on show me the money is to acknowledge how deeply this economic norm is embedded in our psyche and to help us notice how and when we use it. Being a resilient investor requires that we have the flexibility to choose among various strategies, depending on the situation, but we cannot do that if we are not even aware of our habitual responses.

Life was not always this way; and even today there are many indigenous societies and outliers of mainstream culture that have not bought into show me the money as an organizing principle. How did the rich diversity of human motivations, from altruism and empathy, to devotion and service, to love and the Golden Rule all become secondary to the pursuit of wealth? Simply put: it works—or at least it has worked, for lots of people, over the past couple of centuries.

Amid growing prosperity, the ease of going along with the dominant paradigm was one of its great self-sustaining virtues; those who looked beyond the simple bottom line or questioned whether a market economy actually does produce the greatest social good were easily dismissed. As millions of people were lifted from subsistence living, a great body of economic work emerged to justify the dominance of this single-minded approach. Foremost among these precepts is the dictate to trust the market.

For investors and corporations, this unquestioned faith in Adam Smith's "invisible hand" justifies any and all pursuit of private gain, since the precept holds that this is the most efficient route to bring about the greatest good for all. Arguments abound about what Smith really meant and how his ideas play out in a world vastly different from the agrarian times in which he lived.[31] Nonetheless, by focusing on their own gain, most Americans feel assured that they are just doing their part, for the economy and the country as well as for their families and community.

Another legacy of this approach is what we might call "bowing to the bottom line": prioritizing the maximization of profits and the minimization of costs. This bottom-line focus is one that we can all identify with when we put a price on our services or go shopping for the best deal. With this strategy, issues such as how and by whom a product was made, or whether there was an effort to protect the environment or workers, are given lip service or simply ignored.

As show me the money has become more deeply engrained, its effects have become more insidious. David Stockman, who led the Office of Management and Budget under President Ronald Reagan, condemns the "financialization" of our society as "corrosive," turning the economy into a "giant casino."[32] Its extreme excesses, such as the securitization of shaky mortgages, are widely cited as the trigger that precipitated the economic collapse of 2008.

The fundamental reason why we do not include this strategy within the framework of resilient investing is its lack of accountability for the many social, environmental, and even spiritual externalities that show me the money leaves in its wake. These costs may be unintended, but they are nonetheless severe and are indeed borne by governments, the nonprofit sector, and society at large. This blanket neglect of responsibility is why we cannot recommend it as a strategy. Today, with our heightened awareness of the ways in which our personal decisions play into the various crises of our times, it has become more and more difficult to pretend that we can wash our hands of the suffering of others.

On the other hand, we recognize that *all of us* are participants in business as usual; it is unavoidable. We must be mindful of our financial situation, stretch our dollars as much as we can, and make decisions that are smart for ourselves and our families. So although we are concerned— very concerned in fact—that show me the money is exerting a downward pull on a muddle-through scenario, we hold our criticism for the *strategy*, not for those of us who sometimes, or even mostly, have adopted this approach to life.

Fortunately, there are other choices. Our three resilient investment strategies—close to home, sustainable global economy, and evolutionary—all include a built-in ethic that encourages us to balance our financial considerations with a wider range of desired outcomes.

We need to work toward a time when more people feel empowered to make choices that *do* consider the good of society and the world. Every time we go against the grain and invest in ways that are not solely motivated by making the most money, we are helping to do just that.

CHAPTER 4

A Field Guide to
Resilient Investing

A Tour of the Nine Zones of the Resilient Investing Map

Now that you are oriented to the rows and columns of the RIM, you are probably eager to see the colorful variety of investments that are blossoming all across this expanded territory. What do you find in the place where tangible assets chart an evolutionary course, or financial assets come close to home? This section is designed as a field guide, one that will help you recognize some of the species that you will encounter in each of the nine investment zones.

Here is where you'll experience just how rich and vibrant resilient investing can be; the write-ups are packed with detail, providing a solid introduction to the diversity of options available in each zone. As with any field guide, this detail is fascinating but perhaps best taken in small doses; digging in to a couple of these zones in a sitting may give you more than enough to chew on. If so, we suggest that you return to this section periodically. Of course, the book's website fills out every zone in ways we can't fit into a book.

A couple of quick points of context are in order before you dive in. First, the specific options mentioned in each investment zone are just a few of many similar or related opportunities, intended to give the flavor of what can be done there; they should not be seen as specific recommendations. You will want to get to know more of them, and dig deeper, so that you can make an informed choice for yourself about which ones to bring into your resilient investing portfolio. Second, because everything is connected, many of these investments cross over into zones other than the one we put them in. That is to be expected; life is holistic—and messy. In the real world, not everything fits into tidy compartments.

Now, let's start our tour.

ZONE 1
Personal Assets/Close to Home

This first zone is the most intimate realm of investment. It is where we focus on our self, and those closest to us, all within the place we call home. These include investments in your own personal skills and well-being as well as actions that deepen your relationships with family, neighbors, and all those who form your networks of support (even if they don't physically live close to you, they are close to the heart!). Home also includes the natural world around us; getting to know the place where you live is one investment you won't want to miss. These investments help build resilience for you, your family, and your community.

Even more than in the rest of the personal assets row, this zone mostly involves investments of your time rather than money. But remember: time is everyone's most precious resource, so you will want to allocate it wisely. Hobbies, healthy habits, and supplemental skills pay off financially by reducing expenses while also being fun and fulfilling in their own right. These too are investments, providing immediate rewards and paying healthy dividends in the future. This zone is about making conscious choices about how we apply the resource of time and energy to enhancing our personal assets.

These are a few of our favorite things.

Improve Your Health

Invest in yourself in the most intimate way: your own physical and psychological health. As Ralph Waldo Emerson wrote, "The first wealth is health,"[1] and as any sick person will tell you, without your health little else matters. There are so many resources available it's hard to know where to start, and we are investment advisors, not health advisors, so consult your primary care provider and consider diet, exercise, and preventive care as cornerstones of this investment. The time and money you devote now are likely to garner solid returns in the form of increased vitality and reduced healthcare costs later.

Change Your Habits

Habit change is not easy—anyone on a diet can tell you that—but it is often where the biggest returns can be. The best of these investments don't take any money at all and often very little time; all that is required is attention. What does it cost to turn off lights when you leave a room? That's right, it doesn't cost anything! But it results in lower energy bills. Or consider annual gas savings if you go to the grocery store half as often or ride your bike instead of drive. Making minor adjustments to acts of daily living can deliver a high return on investment.

Do It Yourself, Together!

"Do it yourself" (DIY) is integral to the American spirit—the willingness to roll up our sleeves, learn a new skill, and make, not buy, solutions. Learn some basic building or plumbing skills; make sauerkraut or yogurt! We like to add "together" to the individualistic spirit of DIY: join with your family, friends, and neighbors to accomplish something much bigger than anyone can do alone. Join a sewing circle, plant a community garden; have fun, improve your health, and strengthen your social bonds. If you have been paying $8.50 for a small jar of crushed cabbage and salt, you know that these skills can save you money.

Build Community

Small investments of time in community building can garner significant and immediate personal returns (conviviality, inspiration) and possible longer-term benefits (safety and support). Transition Towns and Community Emergency Response Teams (CERTs) are two programs that can help dramatically improve community resilience. Volunteering at local nonprofits and participating in faith communities builds both relationships and community resilience. Knowing concerned and skilled neighbors, working together to address weaknesses in the community, and creating a response plan—Where do we meet up? Can we help one another install emergency water storage?—all help build long-term safety and increase peace of mind.

Close-to-home investments are so pleasing because they easily satisfy other needs: they are fun and they connect you with your community, often across generations. Learning how to knit socks from Nana is a great way to invest a Friday night. These nonfinancial investments in health, heart, and hearth are deceptively powerful, offering returns that are valuable beyond measure. The sense of purpose, satisfaction, connection with land, self, and others—these are all factors that many would cite as what makes life worth living.

ZONE 2
Personal Assets/Global Economy

1	**2**	3
4	5	6
7	8	9

This zone is where you engage with the big wide world, striving to choose actions that can help tip the scales of the global economy toward sustainable outcomes. Investments in this realm largely involve career and lifestyle choices along with opportunities to use your time and energy to influence the shape of society and the economy.

A Meaningful Career

A key place to start is with your career. Does it provide meaning as well as a good living? Would a career change, or simply a change in employer or specific job, offer better alignment between your overall worldview and how you spend the largest part of your days? Making a change is not easy—it can involve a new course of education or relocating, among other challenges—but the emotional and financial rewards might be enormous. Taking the time to design a life in which your work is deeply meaningful[2] pays enormous dividends in personal satisfaction and social betterment and ensures that when you come home from work, you are enthused rather than depleted, with energy to devote to other priorities such as volunteering, family, and exercise.

The Evolving Workplace

Perhaps you already love your job. What can you do within your workplace to change it for the better, both for employees and in terms of the company's relationships with the greater world? The following examples are among the positive changes that you might participate in or help catalyze.

- Start a wellness club, encouraging exercise and perhaps a shared mindfulness or meditation practice.

- Advocate for recycling and the procurement of local, recycled, and biodegradable products—and work to make your company's products more socially and environmentally responsible.

- Engage with your co-workers in community service—on company time!

- Share company expertise with young people and the less fortunate via internships and educational outreach.

- Organize your business as a B Corp[3] or obtain other sustainable business certification such as from Green America or from an industry-specific association.

These types of initiatives can make work more enjoyable and foster pride in your company, which research has shown to have a positive correlation to both quality and profitability.[4]

Lifestyle Choices

Beyond the workplace, there are many other lifestyle choices that shape your participation in the global economy. For starters, the choice of where you live has countless ripple effects: urban dwellers who rely on public transit have among the lowest carbon and other resource footprints, while living and working (including telecommuting) in a rural town offers substantial benefits in both connection with nature and opportunities to participate directly in local governance. Orienting your home and work life to accommodate bikeability turns transportation from a large financial and environmental cost to a significant personal health benefit.

Advocacy: Changing Corporate Citizenship

There are many opportunities for citizens and shareholders to participate in the change that is under way to forge a more responsible approach to corporate citizenship. Now that we have at our fingertips the ability to network with like-minded people and groups throughout the world, you can be part of this change by devoting some of your time to citizen advocacy, whether locally, nationally, or globally.

Shareholders hold particular power to influence corporate policy via proxy voting and working with others to submit resolutions; this has led to Home Depot's no longer selling old-growth timber, FedEx Office's using only recycled copy paper, and McDonald's abandoning polystyrene foam cups.[5] Individuals and companies can join with groups like the American Sustainable Business Council to participate in public policy, engaging with regulatory agencies and Congress to help establish higher standards and expectations for corporate behavior.

ZONE 3

Personal Assets/Evolutionary

The quest to improve the human condition requires clarity of purpose. Are there ways that we can strengthen our personal assets base to become a valued crewmember on the journey? How can we help humanity not only solve our current challenges but also boldly go where no one has gone before?

This zone asks you to focus on improving your ability to notice, engage with, and help create the leading edge of innovation that is bubbling up all over the planet. That's a big task, so to get started we steer you to two main entry points, both of which will open up a lot of new ground to explore: looking inside ourselves, and tuning in to the accelerating advance of knowledge and innovation.

Start from the Inside:
Self-Inquiry and Personal Development

Many with an evolutionary bent focus on changing the economic and social systems that dominate today's world, but the system we are all closest to is our own self. As Gandhi famously said, we must "*be* the change we wish to see in the world." The inner growth spurred in this zone will pay dividends in the clarity and integration of the decisions you make across the RIM, especially (but not only) in the richness of your personal and professional life.

But where to start? Here's an idea: take a walk and ask yourself some probing questions. One we like comes from William McDonough, which he uses to help corporate leaders focus on the central questions of our times: "How can we love all of the children, of all species, for all time?"[6]

Both within and outside established traditions, many are exploring what an "evolutionary spirituality" might look like. As one example, in *Integral Life Practice* Ken Wilber and colleagues describe a fourfold practice that includes body, mind, spirit, and self-reflection. A framework like this can help you identify which areas need the most attention while ensuring that you are touching all the bases. Perhaps this seems out of place in a book about investing, but what we are suggesting is that it's possible to deepen your capacities for clarity and balance and that putting some of your time and even money into these pursuits is both wise and prudent.

Finally, don't forget that we need each other. Doing this kind of inner work can bring up all sorts of questions and challenges, so it is best to have a strong support network, which may include professional counselors or trusted spiritual advisors. The work you do in this zone goes deeper and works faster when shared with others.

Jump into the Future:
Learning and Connecting

One hallmark of evolutionary investors is their commitment to lifelong learning. Of course each of us will have our particular primary and secondary interests; the future will also need many of us to be generalists, making the new connections necessary to move society forward. We live in an era that can overwhelm us with information, so finding reliable filters—whether they are websites, podcasts, authors and journalists, or conferences and classes—will enable you to focus on what is most relevant to you.

Technology is a central player in nearly any scenario, and its pace of change requires ongoing focus to avoid becoming a dinosaur. Innovations like 3D printing and bioengineering are rapidly changing our ideas about what is possible. Even if you are not an early adopter, try to stay aware of new tech and systems that are moving from concept to reality.

Turning to the social opportunities offered in this zone, you will want to find your place in the new forms of online global community that continue to blossom. Your ability to learn from leading thinkers and actors in almost every field—and to share your own leading-edge ideas—has never been greater.

And finally, the nature of work itself is being transformed by the quick pace of innovations; robots and outsourcing are taking a toll on jobs that were once thought to be immune from those pressures. At the same time, the opportunities available to entrepreneurs are limitless. From putting your offerings into the budding sharing economy, to collaborating in open-source global networks, you may find your future profoundly shaped by evolving your own participation in the world.

ZONE 4

Tangible Assets/Close to Home

1	2	3
4	5	6
7	8	9

Here is where we are quite literally bringing it all home. Home is where the heart is, and it's also one of the best areas for making profitable investments. Leveraging your own experience, energy, and sweat equity, along with money you have saved or borrowed, can pay big returns. Investment could be in one's home, in home improvements such as adding an in-law or rental unit to your house, in energy efficiency and renewable energy generation, or for other ends, such as building the physical elements of household and community resilience. Planting a garden is an easy first step, even for renters.

Converting financial assets into tangible assets is the distinctive feature of this zone. You will find plenty of smaller investments that can pay off via reduced expenses. On the other hand, some investments here are the biggest investments many of us will ever make, such as a home. Much of what you do in this basket offers *intangible* rewards such as pride of ownership and accomplishment.

The "Realest" Estate: Home and Home Improvements

Homeownership is one of the primary financial goals for many, and for good reason; it serves countless functions beyond providing a roof over your head. Personal real estate is usually the *most* tangible asset that anyone invests in, while also offering significant tax advantages. But make sure you think carefully about where and how you buy; the physical location and layout of your home plays into many other practical and lifestyle choices you'll be making in the years to come. Add-on units for rental income or for family can add tremendous financial and social value, as can sharing opportunities such as family compounds or cohousing.[7] You could build or buy a "tiny house"[8] or a lovely refurbished Airstream travel trailer and use it for similar purposes. If you have sufficient capital, and ideally some construction skills, investment real estate can be a profitable venture. Evaluate your location and your borrowing terms very carefully.

Energy Efficiency and Renewable Energy Generation

Some of the best returns on investment are available through judicious application of energy efficiency strategies. We all know that adding foam-and-tape weather stripping around doors and windows costs little in cash and just a bit of time but can save hundreds of dollars a year in energy costs while improving comfort. Solar thermal or photovoltaic panels often provide an excellent return on investment as well as protection from rising electricity rates. Think big: whole-systems design can provide dramatic returns on investment by "tunneling through the cost barrier."[9] This involves designs that can end up reducing initial capital costs, such as using enough insulation and air sealing so that a smaller furnace suffices to heat a home.[10]

Shop and Share Locally

Purchasing locally grown and processed foods and goods tends to be more expensive than similar products bought at a big box store, but that differential can be seen as an investment in the resilience and well-being of one's local community. Look for a CSA farm near you, where fresh, local food can be purchased, often at a cost savings.[11] And tap into the sharing economy:[12] you can save money and accomplish more by borrowing from your neighbors—and even make some cash by letting others rent your car or a room in your house.

Community Commons

Putting time and energy, as well as some money, into the shared infrastructure of your community can pay long-term social and tangible returns. Supporting a local land trust, tending a community garden, joining work parties at regional parks or trails, or being part of a team reclaiming intersections or creating "pocket parks" in more built-up areas—all are worthwhile investments. Volunteers serving on town committees and as board members for nonprofits and local water, sewer, or electric companies are all providing a key public service while building strong social relationships as well.

Our earliest investments in the tangible aspects of community can be seen as marking the emergence of humankind; in the modern day, our activities here literally give shape to our civilization. There is great satisfaction to be gained from being able to hold, see, or live within a profitable investment.

ZONE 5

Tangible Assets/Global Economy

1	2	3
4	**5**	6
7	8	9

The center zone on the RIM is indeed the core of our economic lives: shopping! Our activities in this zone offer the opportunity to notice and take responsibility for our consumption of the physical things we need in our lives. While we have become accustomed to having access to consumer goods produced nearly anywhere in the world, how often do we pause to consider the human and environmental impacts created along the way?

The allure and simplicity of participating in the global economy make it all too easy to gloss over the accumulation of unintended consequences that live within that system. Issues such as how and by whom a product was made, or what the environmental consequences might be, are often swept under the rug. Our purchasing decisions offer a chance to rethink some of these consequences and to take some steps toward engaging with the *sustainable* global economy as much as possible, leading to more informed decisions that not only facilitate our own well-being but also contribute to a just and healthy world.

Tangible Purchases

The choices we make as we purchase both consumable items (food and clothing) and durable products (personal electronics, cars, and appliances) all have ripple effects, including impacts on workers and communities, energy used in making and transporting them to us, and environmental consequences of production and disposal. For motivation to consider these impacts more closely, we recommend *The Story of Stuff*, a short film that has been viewed online more than 30 million times.

Scaling back your consumption, which conserves resources and can pay enormous personal and social returns, is the focus of the voluntary simplicity movement. There are countless books[13] and websites[14] featuring strategies for simple living; Joe Dominguez and Vicki Robin's 1992 classic (revised in 2008), *Your Money or Your Life,* is an enduring inspiration.

You can also take advantage of a burgeoning new marketplace to fulfill some of your need for many tangible items. As part of the sharing economy, several corporations—notably Zipcar and Uber—are targeting car ownership. Smaller items are also increasingly being shared through online services and community initiatives such as tool libraries.

When you do purchase products, there are many issues that you might want to consider, from human rights to toxic chemicals to management practices. Tough as it is to be aware of the behaviors and policies of every company (did you know Macy's formally lobbied in Texas against equal pay for women?—in 2013![15]), there are resources that can help, at least for well-known corporate brands. Green America's Responsible Shopper website rates familiar brands on their social, environmental, and management practices, helping identify the best companies in a sector, as well as greener, small-company alternatives; the similar Good Guide developed an associated mobile app[16] with a QR-code reader; you can now scan product bar codes and learn instantly about company ethical standards! Many organizations have created conscious-consumer guides[17] and issue-specific product certifications[18] (see endnote for a list of many of our favorites).

It's also worth seeking out businesses operating with corporate structures that prioritize social and environmental responsibility. Co-ops come in all shapes and sizes, from local groceries to worker-owned contracting companies and continent spanning farmer-owned meat and dairy cooperatives. We are particularly passionate about the benefit corporation movement, which includes B Corp certification and a new legal

class of corporations in nearly two dozen states that requires businesses
to operate for the benefit of people and planet in addition to their owners.

Tangible Investments

A standard hedge against currency devaluation and stock price volatility is
precious metals, with gold and silver leading the category; look for legacy
and fair-trade sources to minimize social and environmental impacts.[19]
Art and collectibles may also offer opportunities to hold (and, if you're
fortunate, gain) value outside the currency and financial markets.

Finally, many traditional investments in tangible property can be
adapted to fit the sustainable model. Investment property that's built
and managed with social and environmental sensitivity (e.g., urban
infill or green-designed commercial property), owning organic farmland
managed by others, and eco-tourism projects—all could fit this bill.

ZONE 6
Tangible Assets/Evolutionary

1	2	3
4	5	**6**
7	8	9

This zone is where we roll up our sleeves and get our hands
dirty. By re-envisioning our relationship with nature and how
we manage the flow of materials and energy, activities in this
area are creating innovative on-the-ground (and in-the-ground) solutions
and opportunities. The tangible assets we are talking about are as familiar
as life itself: trees, livestock, soil, grass, the oceans, and the atmosphere.
But here the goal is to return, to restore, and to regenerate; interdepen-
dency, holism, reciprocity, and diversity are actively woven into the
design. The outcome, "to recreate the Garden of Eden,"[20] is at the heart
of the evolutionary impulse. Applying this strategy to tangible assets is a
profound investment in the foundation of all wealth.

Returning to our roots, literally, but with new eyes and new abili-
ties, "bioneers"[21] are evolving how we can reinvest into natural capital
and reinvigorate all human systems. Even our industrial systems can

be redesigned "to cherish what remains of the earth and to foster its renewal."[22] Let's look at some of what is being worked on.

Digging into Regenerative Agriculture

The aim of this restorative style of agriculture is to align with the amazing fecundity of nature and build a human system around this abundance that benefits people and planet while also turning a profit. As *Slow Money* author Woody Tasch describes it, "We can bring money back down to earth."[23] Here are some exciting projects we love:

- Sustainable woodlots and forestry, like the Menominee Tribal Forest,[24] where a diversity of species, ages, and functions yields a beautiful and functional forest ecosystem for the long term

- Community-level food forests, such as the work done at the Beacon Food Forest in Seattle that grows fruits, nuts, and other supporting plants right in town

- Aquaponics systems, where plants and fish grow together synergistically, the best of hydroponics and aquaculture; the brilliant Urban Farm in Milwaukee[25] is an excellent example

- Planned grazing systems, where domestic animals mimic wild herds and regenerate grasslands as a result; Green Pastures Farm in Missouri is one of many examples[26]

Are there any examples of regenerative agriculture projects like these in your area? If not, find (or start) a Slow Money chapter[27] and work with other interested folks in your community to get something going. Participate in a CSA farm or prepay for larger amounts of produce, meat, or food products, such as on the Credibles model.[20]

Conservation Finance: Restoring an Ecosystem Near You

Many other innovations are tapping into the regenerative power of nature. Conservation finance focuses on fields such as habitat conservation, sustainable forestry, and clean water. Addressing our greatest planetary challenge, the Virgin Earth Challenge, created by Sir Richard Branson, offers $25 million to any organization that can demonstrate a sustainable and economically viable means of removing greenhouses gases from the atmosphere. Investors looking for inspiration will find Allan Savory's Holistic Management among the finalists, along with companies developing biochar, an ancient Amazonian technique that stores carbon while increasing soil fertility. The Nature Conservancy and Ecotrust are two organizations that have created opportunities for accredited investors.

Thinking Like the Earth: Evolving the Circular Economy

The many practical visionaries working in this realm aspire to create well-integrated human systems modeled on nature's wisdom. Permaculture (see chapter 3) offered an early practical foundation, and biomimicry looks to plants and animals for direct design inspiration,[29] such as spiraling conch shells leading to far more efficient propellers and fans. As Katherine Collins, author of *The Nature of Investing: Resilient Investment Strategies through Biomimicry*, says, "Asking, 'What would nature do?' can be the first step toward decisions and designs that are optimized instead of maximized, generative instead of extractive, mindful instead of mechanical."

With this mindset, each step in a process can generate a new yield, a new business opportunity. William McDonough sees red and wriggling vermiculturists (worms to the lay audience) creating soil fertility and adapts this insight into a circular economy approach to the "technical nutrients" of industrial design; as a sign of things to come, you can now return some products to the manufacturer for complete recycling at the end of their useful life.

Decentralized Manufacturing

Extruding (!) onto the scene now, desktop-scale 3D printing revolutionizes the ability to fabricate almost any product, from toys to bikinis to unique widgets.[30] As Jeremy Rifkin asks, "What if millions of people could manufacture batches or even single manufactured items in their own homes or businesses, cheaper, quicker, and with the same quality control as the most advanced state-of-the-art factories on earth?"[31]

The "maker movement"[32] brings together the DIY spirit with technology. It will be years before we see how truly transformative this tangible technology will be, but this is a great time to jump in.

While much of the activity in this basket is not widely available for direct investment outside venture capital firms and angel networks, that is changing. In the meantime find regional projects to get involved in, consider directing some of your charitable giving here, support companies on the vanguard, and keep your eyes open for chances to get your money dirty while doing some good clean work in the world.

ZONE 7

Financial Assets/Close to Home

In a world where $3 trillion circulates through global currency markets every day, it is easy to forget that, until recently, keeping your money close to home was the most ordinary of choices. Banks were locally owned, and entrepreneurs depended on their own connections if they wanted to finance a business. But local communities, and small businesses in particular, find it difficult to tap into today's swirling ocean of cash. Complicating the situation, securities rules devised to protect investors from swindlers make it difficult for small companies to sell ownership shares to the public. Undaunted by the challenges, a hardy cohort of community activists has planted local investment seeds that have grown and thrived here in the United States and globally. As a result, there are now many ways to invest in communities, some of which can be done right from a standard brokerage account; you can even make local investments using your individual retirement account (IRA)!

Let's focus on *your* home community. What if it were possible to shift a significant portion of your financial assets away from Wall Street and onto Main Street—to invest in helping your neighbors find a place to live, create jobs, and improve the local quality of life? Sure, this sounds good in theory, but even opening to this possibility brings up a bevy of practical issues: Could you earn a fair return? Can you diversify so that you are not taking too much risk with any single investment? How would you even find such opportunities?

Get Involved

While the best resource is to network locally, we can point you to some tools and directories. Amy Cortese's *Locavesting: The Revolution in Local Investing and How to Profit from It* and Michael Shuman's *Local Dollars, Local Sense: How to Shift Your Money from Wall Street to Main Street and Achieve Real Prosperity* both do an excellent job of covering the innovations occurring around the United States.

The Local Investing Resource Center is an online hub for collaboration and learning about local investing; and two organizations, Green America and BALLE—the Business Alliance for Local Living Economies—offer community investing guides online.

Banking

In many places, you will discover member-owned credit unions and locally owned banks that are happy to provide you with the same services (savings, checking, CDs) that you might now be getting from a distant corporate bank. Do a little digging to make sure that you understand their mission and what sort of impact they are making in your hometown. While some focus on consumer loans, others are deeply involved in affordable housing or locally owned businesses.

Loan Funds

Beyond the familiar confines of banks and credit unions, you may also discover lesser-known options such as community loan funds, which provide financing for underserved populations. Regional funds are at work in most areas of the United States and offer a safe place for some of your savings; rather than being parked in a CD, your money can be paying substantial social dividends.

Investing in Your Neighbors

Getting even more personal is the possibility of investing in specific local businesses. You can make your own deal directly with the owner, or consider joining a group that brings together investors and local entrepreneurs seeking capital. The Slow Money movement is helping support the creation of investment clubs that focus on farms and food. James Frazier, a Natural Investments financial advisor, co-founded the groundbreaking Local Investing Opportunities Network (LION), which is being replicated in many communities. While investment clubs pool their money and vote on which local or regional projects to invest in, LION groups simply bring the parties together and allow each investor to make his or her own deal with selected businesses.

Woody Tasch gets people thinking by asking, "What would the world be like if we invested 50 percent of our assets within 50 miles of where we live?" It is a great question, with nice round numbers, but it's up to you to decide how much to invest and to define what "close to home" means. Most people will start with modest amounts, increasing as they gain comfort and more opportunities appear. And what's *your* range? For those living in a city, 50 miles might be too expansive when there are needs and opportunities down the street. Out in the country, a larger region might be needed to provide the necessary diversity. What matters most is that you take the time to really get to know where you live, see what the needs are, and find opportunities that speak to your desire to connect your money with the place you call home.

ZONE 8
Financial Assets/Global Economy

This zone of the RIM is where we turn our attention to what most people consider "investing": putting money into a diversified selection of stocks, bonds, mutual funds, and other financial instruments being traded in the global economy. While resilient investing offers us many more baskets to choose from, this zone remains a key place to focus on growing your financial assets.

As you know, we are passionate about engaging the global economy in ways that raise the bar on corporate citizenship. Naturally, much of what we recommend here follows from our 25-plus years in the field of sustainable and responsible investing. We see SRI as a fundamental tool that enables your financial investments to be consistent with all the choices you are making with your time, attention, and money across the entire RIM. In particular, it enables you to align your investment choices with your own values, and by so doing to encourage corporations to change in ways that better serve society and the planet. For most investors these goals are achieved by choosing mutual funds and financial advisors that are as committed as you are to making a positive impact while remaining focused on earning solid financial returns (see Resource 1: The Case for SRI).

Over the past decade, SRI's pioneering integration of social, environmental, and corporate governance considerations has been embraced by much of the mainstream financial-planning industry[33] as well as by institutional investors such as public pensions, religious organizations, labor funds, foundations, and endowments. The United Nations Principles for Responsible Investment, launched in 2006, now has 1,200 signatories representing $34 trillion under management.

Choose Your Criteria

SRI's values alignment is achieved in part using portfolio screening, which avoids investments in companies engaging in activities that are inconsistent with your values while seeking out stocks and bonds from corporations and government programs that are operated in a socially just and environmentally wise manner. Screening has a fascinating, centuries-long history, much of it with faith-based roots. Its modern expression sprung from the peace and environmental movements of the early 1970s, as investors sought to avoid military contractors and major polluters. Since then such "negative screening" has expanded greatly and may include toxic products, repressive regimes, animal testing, lack of transparency on corporate governance issues, and climate change factors.

SRI is sometimes unfairly pigeonholed as being only about avoiding investments, but it also emphasizes positive screens designed to actively seek out companies that perform well on a variety of issues (e.g., prioritizing employee welfare and diversity and minimizing environmental and host community impacts) or companies active in key sectors of the green economy (including organic food, renewable energy, fitness, green building, or access to water). The particular screens used by each fund vary widely, so you should make sure that the issues most important to you are being addressed by the funds you choose. Our company offers a free "Heart Rating" service that rates more than 120 funds.

Activism

The second goal—raising the bar on what we expect from corporate citizenship—is accomplished by engaging in shareholder activism and policy development at the state and national levels. If this is important to you, you will want to choose companies and/or mutual funds that are making positive contributions in these realms.

SRI mutual funds, along with progressive institutional investors, begin by engaging company management in dialogue. This often leads to substantive policy changes, such as the development of sustainability policies and reports (Costco), protection of human rights and safe working conditions (Disney), and product recycling (Apple). When dialogue fails, broader pressure is applied via shareholder resolutions. On the policy front, your investment in these players will support ongoing efforts to improve Securities and Exchange Commission rules and to engage Congress and government agencies on a wide variety of social and environmental issues.

A final thought: The long-term investing we undertake in this zone is often aimed toward fulfilling some future plan or dream—funding our kids' education or our own retirement, moving to a nicer home, being able to travel a bit. These sorts of goals remind us that we are not investing in the global economy simply for the sake of having more money; we're looking forward to the promise of the future. Who wants to retire on a polluted, war-torn planet? By directing your investments in this zone using SRI criteria, you are putting your bets on your own dreams and on a better future for all.

ZONE 9

Financial Assets/Evolutionary

1	2	3
4	5	6
7	8	9

We saved the biggest leap for last. Here we are putting our money where our vision is, seeking out game-changing projects and companies. It's an exciting quest, where you will encounter some of the world's most innovative thought leaders and hopeful solutions. Evolutionary financial investments are not just about making the best of today's global economy; they are about changing the game.

Today the innovation that's closest to what we are describing is coalescing around impact investing. This is the idea of using money not only to achieve a financial return but also to have a beneficial social and environmental impact. At first we were reluctant to utilize this new term, as all investments have impacts (and they are often not positive). But this framework has ignited the passions of a wide range of investors, with interest in such areas as microfinance, renewable energy, low-income housing, and job creation.[34] It is thrilling to see how this idea is attracting millions of dollars (and aiming for billions) from large Wall Street firms,[35] making it possible for evolutionary ideas to scale up.

Unfortunately, due to a jumble of laws intended to protect smaller investors, today's range of evolutionary financial investments is rather limited unless you qualify as an accredited investor, which generally means that you have more than $1 million in net worth or earn more than $200,000 per year. But change is afoot, and even today there are several viable avenues on which nonaccredited investors can explore their evolutionary impulses.

- Crowdfunding laws are starting to make room for smaller investors to buy into evolutionary startups.

- The sharing economy is a recent disruptive innovation that is changing patterns of consumption and concepts of ownership while opening up new forms of livelihood.

- Peer-to-peer lending sites such as Prosper and Lending Club are cutting out big banks by enabling people to make loans to one another.

- Shared office and micromanufacturing hubs[36] are sprouting up in cities and towns, reducing the barriers for ordinary people to start their own businesses.

Among the most exciting new opportunities in this realm are crowdfunding projects that enable investors to collaboratively own solar photovoltaic energy systems that variously serve large users (hospitals, condos, schools), benefit underserved communities, or are locally owned projects in the investors' own community. The users lock in a lower fixed utility rate while the investor recoups the capital investment and generates income for up to 20 years. Mosaic led the way, and many other companies[37] are now offering investments in solar financing.

A more mature field in this realm is community investing, which aims to serve the needs of those who fall through the cracks of the current financial system. In the discussion of zone 7, we spoke about some ways to invest close to home. But you can also seek out community investments that are close to *other* people's homes, all over the world. Community investing is perhaps the best way to participate in evolutionary investments if you do not have a large bankroll.

The Calvert Foundation has made it easy for any investor, with only a $1,000 minimum, to put money into a wide range of projects through its Community Investment Notes. They can be purchased directly, or through most brokerage firms, which means you can hold them in an IRA. They have been rock solid, with a spotless repayment track record. Kiva is a site that lets you invest small amounts and choose a developing-world loan recipient directly. With today's minuscule interest rates on savings and CDs, you may even find opportunities to earn a slightly higher return while your money does good deeds in the world.

If you *do* qualify as an accredited investor, you will want to keep abreast of the fast-changing world that is coalescing under the impact investing framework. There are more and more ways for you to find venture investments in cutting-edge companies and funds[38] that are seeking solutions to today's most intractable challenges and pioneering new ways to meet human needs. From distributed energy to vertical farming, 3D printing to ecovillages, you will find many intriguing opportunities.

This whirlwind tour only scratches the surface. New currency innovations like Bitcoin are changing the way we think about money, let alone investing! As with all the assets using the evolutionary strategy, it's important to stay aware of the latest news and developments.

CHAPTER 5

Find Yourself on the Map

What You Are Already Doing: Self-Assessment

Now that you have a full picture of the resilient investing framework, it's time to learn how to put these concepts to work in your life. In this chapter you'll be assessing where your current actions fit on the Resilient Investing Map and begin thinking about how your own priorities and life situation can find expression within our expanded view of investing. While the RIM may seem fundamentally new, you have undoubtedly been making investments for many years that can be plugged right into your personal map.

For example, we are guessing that you already devote time each week to your familial, social, and community relationships. Great! You're investing in zone 1. Do you periodically plug in to online social networks or take personal or professional training courses? Check, zone 3. We know you buy stuff, from cereal to cell phones: zone 5. Gardening? Zone 4. Have you supported an interesting new project on Kickstarter or Kiva? Hip hip, you're at work in zone 9! If you chose your job or career in part because it makes a positive contribution to the world, then zone 2 is in play, too.

Of course, simply having some activity in many different zones is not what this is all about; resilient investing is a dynamic process of making clear, conscious choices about *how much* time and money to spend in your activities across the entire RIM. The next two chapters will help you think more deeply about these choices, and chapter 8 will take you through the process of designing your resilient investing plan.

For now we will guide you through the first step: putting your existing investments onto a blank RIM. We prefer to do our brainstorming old-school style, with pen and paper, but you might be the type to crank out a spreadsheet or fill out a document online; the book's website provides a variety of free downloadable resources to assist you in your planning, including a customizable Excel spreadsheet and Word document and the Resilient Investing Map as a PDF or JPG file. But we prefer the tangibility of paper. Give it a try: take out a piece of paper and divide it into a 3 × 3 grid—or, even better, spread out on a big table and use nine sheets, one for each zone on the RIM.

You will be working your way around the map, jotting down anything you are already doing in your life that seems related to each of the nine zones. Simply capture the first few things that come to mind in each zone; there will be plenty of time to add more later. If you don't have anything significant in some of the zones, that's fine too; this might be a clue about areas to focus on later.

To jump-start your inventory, let's consider a few of the things you may put in each zone. Bear in mind that these are just representative examples of the kinds of things you may ask yourself and are far from comprehensive; it may help to refer back to chapter 4 for reminders about each zone. You will likely notice that some things do not fit neatly into a single zone; set the ambiguity aside for now and feel free to list these things in more than one zone or to just make one choice for starters.

Listing Your Assets by Zone

Let's begin with your personal assets. List the things that belong in **zone 1**, personal assets/close to home. What investments are you currently making locally to build your personal/social assets? How is your health? Your community engagement? Your connection with family, biological or chosen?

In **zone 2**, personal assets/global economy, how would you characterize your career? Is it a key piece of your life path that is really humming along? If it is dominating your time but sapping your energy, note that here. Perhaps you are in transition and looking to pick up some new skills.

Next consider your personal and spiritual growth. How would you rate them for **zone 3**, personal assets/evolutionary?

Now repeat this process with the ways you engage with your tangible assets across the three columns, starting with **zone 4**, tangible assets/ close to home. Do you own a home? Have you made investments into the house or landscape? If you are not a homeowner, what about other close-to-home and tangible assets you have invested in, such as being part of community projects that provide tangible benefit for many?

For **zone 5**, tangible assets/global economy, what about your stuff, cars, and equipment? Most of us have significant spending in the global economy; are you happy with your spending patterns and how conscious your choices have been?

For **zone 6**, tangible assets/evolutionary, have you made any investments in sustainable agriculture or conservation finance? Perhaps you're a member of a local collaborative technology center. Don't worry if you have little to report here; this is a very new investment category.

Your financial assets start with **zone 7**, financial assets/close to home. Do you have any accounts in local credit unions, banks, or direct investments in other community projects?

You may already have statements from an accountant or financial planner or records of your own; most of these investments go in **zone 8**, financial assets/global economy. If you don't know where you stand with your financial assets, that's okay, too, but note that you will want to look at this area later. There's no need to list all of your market investments right now; just note whether you have some and whether they are managed using sustainability criteria.

As for **zone 9**, financial assets/evolutionary, this is where you place any impact investments that aim to foster real breakthroughs.

Okay, now that you have completed your first pass, keep it handy, as we will be working through the map again at the end of the chapter.

From here on out, we will be sprinkling in examples of completed RIMs to illustrate how to fill them out. All of them are necessarily abridged, featuring just a highlight or two in each zone.

Case Study: Dahlia the Driver

Dahlia is a recent college graduate who is just starting out. Her father died when she was little, and although her mother was very loving and worked hard, financial strain in the home was high. Dahlia has always been driven to build a better life for herself, deciding early on that she would go to college. She did get some scholarships and graduated from a solid university, but like many students today she ended up with substantial loan debt. SEE FIGURE 3 She has few financial assets and not many tangible

THREE CORE INVESTMENT STRATEGIES			
	Close to Home	**Sustainable Global Economy**	**Evolutionary**
Personal/ Social	**1** Mature interpersonal skills Athletic/healthy	**2** College degree Just starting career in IT	**3** Regular yoga classes Backpacking trips with friends
Tangible	**4** Minimal	**5** Older Toyota Corolla Apple MacBook Smartphone	**6** Minimal
Financial	**7** Minimal savings in local bank	**8** No assets Significant debt from college loans	**9** Minimal share ownership in small company she works for

(Left vertical label: THREE KINDS OF ASSETS / TYPES OF RETURN)

Figure 3 *Dahlia's Inventory RIM*

assets either. Her zone 1 is pretty substantial, with inspiring and supportive friends both near and far and healthy relationships with her mother and siblings. She is just getting started in her career, so she has not yet built up much of an asset base in zone 2, though her college education in a dynamic field is an advance payment on that zone.

Going Deeper: Readying for Resiliency

Let's set the map aside for a moment and add a couple of bigger-picture perspectives to your toolkit. They both address some of the new types of thinking that our system asks of you and will help you engage with more clarity as you go forward.

Your Assets and Personal Predilections

To make the map your own, you will need to consider some deeper questions about who you are and what you have been doing. Your focus here will be on the rows of the RIM—the three asset classes defined in chapter 2. You will be assessing your life situation, along with your personality and goals. The new directions you choose for your path forward will be shaped by your available assets and overall life priorities, so it is crucial to get a clear and realistic picture of what you have to work with. You might want to make some notes as you think through the questions that follow. If any new investment ideas come to mind along the way, start a separate list of these; they will be a starting point in chapter 8 as you compile a comprehensive set of new options for your resilient investing plan.

Personal Assets

- Do you enjoy social engagement, or are you more of a private person?

- Is your time largely accounted for by family or work obligations, or do you have discretionary time that you could devote to new things?

- As you have learned about resilient investing, have you thought about things into which you would like to put more time?

- How important to you is growing your personal assets? This includes family time, deeper connections with friends and colleagues, and emotional/spiritual inquiry.

- What are your skills, talents, and capacities?

Tangible Assets

- Do you already own a home? If so, does it fulfill your needs and desires?

- Do you want to settle in one place, or do you envision moving periodically?

- Do you enjoy expressing yourself through tangible stuff? This includes things like wardrobe, book/music collection, and gadgets.

- Do you have hobbies that require tangible support? Examples include sewing, woodworking, biking, and restoring antique furniture or classic cars.

- What tangible assets are you most interested in growing? This includes home/land/tools, becoming more conscious as you shop for food and other consumable products, and the physical landscape and the natural resources in your region.

Financial Assets

- Do you have financial assets to invest?

- Do you have income that does, or could, allow you to set aside money to invest?

- How important to you is increasing your income and growing your financial assets?

- Would you like to shift some of your existing financial assets or direct some of the money in your monthly budget toward strategically growing your personal or tangible assets?

Your self-assessment and your final resilient investing plan are both shaped in fundamental ways by the specifics of your life. Friends, loved ones, financial advisors, and spiritual or psychological counselors can be invaluable allies as you dig into this process of working with the *entire* map. We encourage you to find some areas to explore that push you out of your comfort zone as you move ahead; taking risks is one of the first steps toward charting a new course for your life. And who knows, you might just find that resilient investing helps you to discover new passions, new ways to be of service, and new opportunities for cultivating love, knowledge, and deeper satisfaction in your life.

Evaluating Nonfinancial Returns

As you have evaluated your investments in each zone, you have likely noticed that there are different types of returns, depending on whether you are investing time, attention, or money in the activity. It is generally straightforward to track your returns on financial investments, but learning how to think about your returns on personal or tangible assets is a bit trickier.

Some tangible assets have concrete financial benefits, often with nonfinancial returns that add to their value: two obvious big-ticket examples are solar panels and a car that gets high gas mileage. Similarly, making a lifestyle choice that minimizes private automobile use in favor of public transit, walking, and biking offers a ripple effect of positive returns: quantifiable financial savings (on gas and car maintenance) as well as a smaller carbon footprint, better health, and more social interaction along the way.

Growing a garden offers a particularly rich opportunity to explore the mix of returns that often result from investment of time: you will save money at the store or farmers market, you will savor the pleasure of physical work and the beauty of mornings in the garden with family and friends, and you will gain the satisfaction of eating fresh, healthy food that you grew yourself. At the end of your second year, you'll want to consider whether the time you devoted to the garden did in fact pay off in the ways you expected, or if there are other things calling for your time.

Similar reflection will be necessary as you look at any other investments related to your personal and tangible assets—and even some of the investments in the financial assets row that are designed to have social or environmental returns, such as involvement in local businesses in zone 7 and impact investing in zone 9.

The returns from your nonfinancial investments are generally subjective; for example, exercise makes you stronger and more energetic; it may also make you feel more self-confident and outgoing. Despite this ambiguity, you can still make a habit of reviewing how well your nonfinancial investments perform compared with your expectations for them. If approached with honesty and care, these assessments provide an essential perspective that you can use to inform your allocations of personal and tangible assets over the years.

A First Look Ahead: Stop/Start/Sustain

Now that you have taken an initial pass through your map and considered some of the larger context of the resilient investing system, take another look at what you have written. What stands out? Highlight anything in your notes from the previous sections that you want to carry over into your final resilient investing plan in chapter 8.

One quick and easy method for completing this early thinking about your activities across the map is the stop/start/sustain technique. For the zones in which you have made investments, do you want to *stop* making those investments, perhaps *start* something new, or *sustain* your current investments? Artistic types might use different colors: black for the inventory, a red line to indicate stopping an investment, perhaps a purple star for investments you want to increase or start, and a green circle for those investments you want to continue. Of course, simple plusses or minuses work too. Don't let a method, or a lack of one, slow you down.

Let's take a look at how another prospective resilient investor completed her map, including her stop/start/sustain intentions (remembering again that your full assessment will likely be more detailed).

As you will see, she is using the +/− method to indicate zones in which she wants to increase or cut back her investment.

Case Study: Adele Adaptability

Adele has always dreamed of making the world a better place. For the past several years, she has spent thousands of dollars on workshops, retreats, and cutting-edge conferences. Established in her career as an environmental attorney, she admits that she's finding the work a little boring these days (zone 2). **SEE FIGURE 4** She is well invested in transformative education (zone 3) and is actively seeking opportunities in the most cutting-edge technologies and ideas (zone 9). She even subscribes

	THREE CORE INVESTMENT STRATEGIES		
	Close to Home	**Sustainable Global Economy**	**Evolutionary**
Personal/ Social	**1** Athletic/healthy Lots of friends and family	**2** **−** JD, admitted to bar in CA, TX, and NY Successful and established career at Dewey, Dino, and Kale	**3** **−** Regular yoga and meditation classes Attends a healing or personal growth workshop once a month Attends TEDx conferences
Tangible	**4** **+ +** Owns home	**5** Substantial spending in this area Toyota Prius Lots of tech and music equipment	**6** Community-supported agriculture farm subscription
Financial	**7** CDs and checking at local bank Community loan fund	**8** Substantial SRI investments in 401(k) Brokerage account at Schwab	**9** Global community loan fund Private placements in renewable energy companies

(left axis label: THREE KINDS OF ASSETS/TYPES OF RETURN)

Figure 4   *Adele's Stop/Start/Sustain RIM*

to a CSA farm (zones 4 and 6). She has SRI mutual funds in her 401(k) (zone 8), while her commitment to social justice leads her to put a big chunk of her savings in local and global community loan funds (zones 7 and 9). She's a diligent health food shopper and drives a hybrid car (zone 5). She owns her home, though she is so busy with work that she hasn't put much energy into it.

~

In these initial passes through your map, you have likely found that you are already doing quite a lot. And we're sure you are itching to get into the juicy task of actually making new plans and reshaping your map for the coming years. Not so fast! To build the personal and societal resilience we have been talking about, you will need to step back from your current patterns and activities and take a closer look at both yourself and our world. We will deepen our explorations in chapter 6, offering some tools and perspectives that are bound to broaden your horizons.

CHAPTER 6

Be Ready for Anything

Qualities of the Resilient Investor,
Scenario Planning, and Plausible Futures

R EADY FOR ANYTHING. TO SOME THAT MAY SOUND DAUNTING, WHILE others hear a clarion call to great adventure. It is a bit of both, harkening to the old saying (some say curse), *May you live in interesting times.* Clearly, the complexity and the uncertainty of our times are handing this to us in spades!

While the preliminary work you just completed is a good start, cultivating resilience requires much more than simply marching ahead with slight tweaks to what you're already doing. This chapter asks you to pause for a moment and prepare for the work at hand by enhancing your internal and external perspectives in ways that allow you to be open and responsive to whatever may come. We are not suggesting that you need a totally clean slate, but you do have the opportunity to take a fresh look at your life, your worldview, and your investments.

We begin this deeper dive by looking inward at the personal qualities that can foster a resilient response to life's opportunities and challenges. Being ready for anything requires flexibility and centeredness; we will point you toward mindsets and practices that may help you to face the challenges with confidence.

Then we'll soar high for a bird's-eye view of the four scenarios that we previewed in chapter 1 to see how the "interesting" aspects of today's world could play out. Clear-minded consideration of the full spectrum of possible futures is an essential first step in building an effective resilient investing plan. In the chapters that follow, you'll use your own assessment of these possible futures to help guide the design of an investment plan that both reflects your personal priorities and prepares you to nimbly respond as needed to any surprises that may come your way.

With all this terrain to cover, it's going to be quite a ride. Are you ready?

Qualities of the Resilient Investor

Yield and you need not break,
Bent you can straighten,
Emptied you can hold,
Torn you can mend;
And as want can reward you
So wealth can bewilder.
Aware of this, a wise man has the simple return
Which other men seek.

—Tao Te Ching, Verse 22, Witter Bynner[1]

We know several high-level martial artists who physically embody the principles and qualities of resilience. We can see them in our mind's eye, and perhaps sharing these images with you will help illustrate the essence of resilience.

Imagine a martial artist standing before you, upright but not stiff or rigid, completely relaxed and at ease. The face is calm and without tension or anger. The eyes are open and soft, not focused on any one thing but seeing anything that might be coming—*10,000-direction eyes,* in martial arts–speak. When attackers approach, our martial artist becomes even more relaxed, moving easily, staying fluid and loose, avoiding strikes and kicks most of the time. Nobody's perfect, so when strikes land, our agile artist absorbs them with breath and flexibility, always moving; head loose and rotating; eyes clear but not focused on a single point, seeing the whole room; light on the feet, advancing and retreating in a dance with the attackers. And then there are more challengers, and the artist stays calm and collected, breathing faster now but still softly, moving with gentle precision, landing blows in unanticipated places with no forced logic or obvious reason (and all the more devastating for it), weaving and dodging, able to go softly to the ground when caught by a blow, to roll and return to balance, to move where forces lead—to be led but also to not lose one's center and grounding and bodily alignment and structure, moving, never settling in a rigid position but staying flexible and in motion to minimize shock and to keep seeking a better position.

Can you feel a bit of the kinesthetic experience we are describing?

This dynamic centeredness and responsiveness gets to the heart of what it means to engage our world in ways that foster resilience. Tomorrow's most successful investors will spend these times surveying the terrain, seeking out the most promising new directions, and poised to adapt to new challenges. Because this landscape is ever changing, investment pathfinders will need a high degree of flexibility and versatility. To do this you will want to reflect on, and strengthen, your inner resources. The resilient mindset does not emerge fully formed; it arises from a range of subtler perspectives that, taken together, provide the clarity and focus you will need in order to thrive as a resilient investor. While inner growth can take many forms, the following are a few key qualities that we have found to be essential.

Hold Multiple Perspectives at Once

Perhaps the central trait of the resilient investor is the ability to consider multiple perspectives about the future—our martial artist's 10,000-direction eyes. The gaze of the resilient investor is soft and open, catching small changes at the periphery, pulling insight from all angles, detecting vectors and changes over time, operating in an expanded sphere that encompasses far more than simply focusing on what is directly at hand. The goal is to be aware of what is really happening, with eyes unclouded by our own tendencies to see what we *want* to see—a common blind spot that sociologists refer to as confirmation bias.

Indeed the perspective that is most challenging to loosen your grip on is the one you find most convincing. Being too sure of what we know, what we believe, or what we feel can make us miss the hints and clues that might have guided us toward a more nuanced perspective or a natural evolution of our worldview over time. It is crucial to draw on the innate human capacity of empathy to remain open to points of view that are entirely different from one's own. You will find that your own perspective is actually *enhanced* if it includes some contradictory possibilities as well as questions that you continue to hold over time. Think of this as having a diverse ecosystem of viewpoints or worldviews.

Comfort with Ambiguity: It's Okay to Not Know

Not knowing what is coming is a fact of life; the resilient investor always keeps this in mind and strives to be comfortable with ambiguity. It's a humbling stance, but it keeps us from getting rigidly attached to any particular outcome. This frees us to think in terms of probabilities rather than certainties, knowing that the complexity of our times will present us with events that cannot be predicted. Someday we may find ourselves confronting a full-on crisis (societal or personal); the martial artist will respond to these times with equanimity—maintaining a calm observer's stance—and even a readiness to let go of ideas, plans, or assets that have been rendered moot by the changes taking place.

Frugality Is Fundamental

You won't see a martial artist expending unnecessary energy or putting up a showy front. Likewise a resilient investor maintains a steady focus on an efficient and well-directed use of resources. The more you can limit or shrink your expenditures, the more options you have. One inspiration for this is Buckminster Fuller's concept of "ephemeralization," which suggests seeking to do more and more with less and less. How can you continuously improve your quality of life with less need for income and less need for new physical stuff? While frugality will give you increased flexibility and choices going forward, it is also a socially and environmentally resilient response to the resource stresses of our time. Your personal commitment to live lightly reflects care for both the needs of others and the health of the ecosystem.

Know a Little about a Lot and a Bunch about a Bit

Generalists will thrive in uncertain futures with a diverse toolkit that can be put to work as needed. The more broad and diverse your understanding of the world, the more you will be attuned to and prepared for the unexpected changes that could come your way. At the same time, becoming highly competent in one or a few areas ensures both that you are employable and that you have skills or knowledge that will be valuable in your community in any possible future. Combining the two is a cornerstone of being educated and ready to play a constructive role in society. The watchful martial artist stays curious and receptive, continually scanning the horizon in all directions for useful information while honing the skills needed to be of service.

Engage!

A martial artist aims to "come out alive," ready to keep moving the situation forward in a positive way. So too the resilient investor stays focused and intent, makes nuanced decisions with clear purpose, and avoids getting stuck in habitual motion or at uncertain rest. By maintaining a dynamic engagement with the surroundings as they change—even in the midst of swirling possibilities and temporary setbacks—we cultivate the creative potential of resiliency, the ability not only to roll with a punch but to put oneself in position to go on the offensive. This quality emphasizes the virtues of having a strong vision of where you want to go and taking decisive steps to get there.

Centering Practice and Self-Awareness

All the qualities we outline here require a fair amount of diligence and focus to cultivate. Our own gradual embrace of these principles has been supported by each of our (very different) ways of prioritizing the development of our innermost resources. Over the course of a life, some combination of counseling, spiritual practice, participation in men's or women's groups, membership in a church community, professional development programs that include an emotional/reflective element, and extended immersions in the natural world with like-minded friends will serve to deepen your self-awareness and help clarify all the choices that present themselves to you.

While it is possible to foster this quality purely on your own by force of attention, most of us find that some sort of emotional or spiritual practice, group, or guidance is invaluable, both as a space in which to engage in more-reflective modes and as a way of staying honest with ourselves about just how "together" we really are. Plumbing our psychological and emotional depths helps us become more aware of the inner dynamics that often drive our habitual responses to events; and cultivating one or several activities that feed our hearts and souls can help lift us up out of conditioned responses and fears and into a place where love and a creative, passionate, and, yes, resilient life can prosper.

It also helps to commit to daily or weekly routines that offer a time for reflection and to quiet your inner chatter. For many a daily workout session or walk to start or end the day serves this purpose. Meditating regularly, even for short periods, is a readily accessible option that can be quite easily incorporated into one's day. Weekend excursions to nearby parks, rivers, or trails are a more casual way to make time for integration. Whether or not you see yourself as on a spiritual path, some sort of mindfulness practice or centering ability is an essential tool for navigating the complex terrain we're sketching out in this book.

∾

We hope that this menu of qualities has given you a taste of what it takes to be an agile, resilient investor. You need not become a black belt, but any effort you make toward developing these attributes will be amply rewarded.

Now there is just one more perspective we want to introduce before you start filling in your map. This one involves a bit of time travel. We will use both our observational skills and our imaginations to paint some pictures of the various ways that things could look in the not-so-distant future, laying out a few broad possibilities along a spectrum that ranges from darker to brighter futures. Later, as you're deciding how much to allocate to each of the resilient investing strategies, you will be guided in part by the likelihood that you assign to each of the possibilities along that spectrum.

Surprisingly, even though investing is obviously about achieving a goal in the future, many investors neglect this crucial step, leaving them vulnerable to their own unseen biases. This is a chance for you to become familiar with your own views about the future and to ask yourself some challenging questions that you might not have grappled with lately, or perhaps at all. By investing time in this exercise, you will find that your capacities for resilience will be greatly enhanced, and you will avoid some shocks and improve your ability to withstand others.

Pick a Future, Any Future

Throughout this book we have frequently made reference to the complexity, uncertainty, and unpredictability of the times in which we live. But we have not provided much backup support for that point of view. This is by design. We know that many of you have already come to the same conclusion we have through your own study and observation of current events, and that others will intuitively see and embrace this description of our world. The focus of this book is to offer proactive solutions (*everyone knows the problem—tell us what we can do!*), so we decided not to divert into the theoretical grounding that underlies these claims. The book's website features our take on this "Story of Our Times," drawing from a wide variety of fields, including complexity science, sociobiology, futurism, new economic theories, and many others.

Suffice it to say, there is an increasingly broad consensus that in today's world we truly *do* need to be ready for anything. There are simply too many compounding issues rippling through our complex civilization that throw a veil of uncertainty over any attempts to predict our path with confidence. Now more than ever, we need some way to make wise decisions to best position ourselves for whatever future may come to pass. The first step is to take a solid look at all the possible scenarios without prefiltering based on how probable or preferable they are to you.

No one presumes that the future will be a clear-cut "victory" for any one of these possibilities; it is far more likely that the actual future will blend aspects of two or more. Indeed elements of all four scenarios are evident in today's world—and, as you will see, many of the specific strategies we introduce in coming chapters can be used as cogent responses to two or more of our plausible futures.

The primary reason why we are asking you to take the time to consider these scenarios a bit more deeply before starting to make your plans is that *resilient investors never go all in on any single worldview*. Relying on the martial artist's 10,000-direction eyes, you will be planning for what you perceive to be the most likely path forward, while monitoring possible challenges from the periphery and staying nimble enough to respond as needed to changing conditions. Consider the next several pages to be a vigilant gaze at the world around you, setting the stage for the responses you'll craft in chapters 7 and 8.

So without putting off the future any longer, let's introduce the contestants in our global scenario sweepstakes. Each has been widely championed by its own camp of serious thinkers; we include a sampling of their perspectives in our summaries and online.

Breakdown, "The Long Emergency"

Social, economic, and/or environmental meltdown,
leaving the global economy in tatters

A book by James Howard Kunstler of the same name[2] describes an extended period of scarcity and structural collapse. Society breaks down in a combination of cascading environmental and economic/sociopolitical catastrophes, unleashing untold suffering and chaos. As the engine of economic growth collapses, the environment has a chance to recover some of its wildness. Humans reorganize into communities that start from scratch, growing their own food, constructing primitive local energy systems, and forming regional economies with local currencies, lots of bartering, and limited trade between regions. Governance takes place close to home, with national and transnational institutions losing clout. While there are many versions of this scenario, each sees the apparent solidity of modern life as a gigantic house of cards; a crisis in just a few key areas of vulnerability could cause the entire house to tumble.

Despite Hollywood's love affair with dystopian futures, those who take these possibilities seriously are often considered to be on the fringes of society. This started to change when Jared Diamond's 2005 book *Collapse: How Societies Choose to Fail or Succeed* brought thinking about this scenario to a more mainstream audience. Knowing that other great civilizations have fallen into chaos provides an alarming wake-up call and has forced even optimists to acknowledge that some version of breakdown is plausible. "Preppers"—those who stockpile food and guns—are the stereotyped image of those who think breakdown is likely. Others, such as many deep ecologists, take a more constructive approach and are working to prepare healthy foundations for local and regional economies and society.[3]

Muddle through

Status quo structures of the global economy endure, oscillating between periods of recession and modest growth

Compared with the economic cliff of breakdown, a muddle-through scenario is a world of slippery slopes and constrained growth. The term *muddle-through economy* was popularized by financial writer John Mauldin in 2002 to describe an economy that is growing but far below what we were accustomed to in the twentieth century, an economy "that would move forward burdened with the heavy baggage of old problems while facing the strong headwinds of new challenges."[4]

We have already seen how extreme weather events (Hurricane Sandy), environmental catastrophes (Fukushima, BP Gulf spill), debt implosions (Eurozone), political instability (Syria, Ukraine), social strains due to wealth inequality (Occupy Wall Street), and other unforeseen factors trigger a crisis response. In the breakdown/long emergency scenario, these push us over the edge; but in a muddle-through scenario, the core elements of our current world continue to function. Enough people are still getting their basic needs met, so despite severe wealth inequality social unrest does not topple dominant governance and corporate structures. Voices calling for fundamental shifts in thinking about the principles that underlie the economy and our political system continue to be marginalized. We still have a habitable and recognizable world governed by strong nation-states, with an economy dominated by global corporations.

Muddling is of course an apt description for the world we have been living in since at least the end of the dot-com bubble. While not ignoring the possible preludes to breakdown/breakthrough that are also in our midst, it seems the most likely scenario to dominate in the short term, though its prospects over longer time frames are uncertain. Within the broad swath of muddling possibilities, it will eventually become apparent if we are moving in a direction that addresses our fundamental challenges.

Therefore we treat muddle through as two separate scenarios, which we call muddle through down and muddle through up.

GLOBAL SCENARIO 2
Muddle through down, "Relentless Struggle"

Rolling recessions amid a failure to address the systemic causes of environmental, social, and economic decline

Ignoring a glut of flashing indicators and scientific consensus warning us of our plight, and despite the fact that we have a wealth of solutions available to help us, we fail to mount a meaningful response to our economic, social, governance, and environmental challenges. We don't hit the wall of systemic collapse, but life becomes a harder struggle for most, as we lurch between abrupt downturns (like we had in 2008) and periods of relative stability.

In this scenario lip service continues to be paid to serious issues such as climate change, even as we double down on a carbon-fueled energy path. Those who hold disproportionate power in today's political/corporate economy pull out all the stops to maintain control, kicking the can down the road rather than putting forth any serious initiatives to address the root causes of our deteriorating situation. Global wealth inequality and marginalized populations fan the flames of conflict, spurring outbreaks of revolt; individual freedoms are whittled away in the name of security, and precious resources are disproportionately allocated to the military at the expense of human needs.

GLOBAL SCENARIO 3
Muddle through up, "Incremental Progress"

Gradual improvement of key quality-of-life indicators within the status quo framework of political and economic systems

We deploy our capacities to their highest effectiveness, making needed improvements and reforms to our existing systems. This moves us steadily toward a prosperous, sustainable future. The late energy activist Randy

Udall proclaimed that the motto for this scenario should be *We have not yet begun to fight! If we faced our challenges head up, with some discipline and focus and political unity, we could still do great things.*[5]

Paul Gilding, author of *The Great Disruption*, concurs, seeing a World War II–type mobilization (*all hands on deck!*) to tackle climate change, as it becomes apparent that the cost of inaction is higher than the cost of restructuring our energy and transportation systems. But all is not necessarily rosy; futurist Jamais Cascio calls this path "walking the tightrope," noting that our eventual success at living within the planet's limits may depend on more-coordinated government planning and that our tardy climate response may necessitate some applications of geo-engineering to forestall the severest damage to the earth's ecosystems.[6]

By pulling together and using all the tools at our disposal, we eventually address our most pressing challenges and find ways to keep the historical arc of global prosperity moving upward. Governments find a way to rise above gridlock. Corporations continue to take incremental steps toward becoming responsible global citizens, giving consideration to social and environmental factors alongside the financial ones. Technological innovations expand access to clean energy and clean water in the developing world, while developed nations become much more efficient. Nations realize that security is more likely to come through fostering education, healthcare, and democracy while addressing global poverty head-on. The climate situation, population pressures, and other environmental concerns continue to worsen for a time, but gradually we work our way toward balance.

GLOBAL SCENARIO 4

Breakthrough, "Rational Emergence"

Exponential social innovation, new technologies, and the evolution of wisdom/consciousness to deploy them wisely

In this twist on Alan Greenspan's famous "irrational exuberance" utterance, humanity embraces the future by unleashing its full potential of creativity and innovation on the economic, political, and social spheres of society. The result is a world that includes technological wonders but also a responsible, respectful connection to the life-support systems of the planet.

Where this scenario breaks from muddling through up is that here we seize the initiative to reinvent social structures that have outlived their usefulness. The emergence of new forms of organization is the essence of evolution in both life and society; it would indeed be rational for us to adapt our ways of doing things to meet the new demands of our time.

If our reliance on debt-based currency and ever-expanding (i.e., infinite) growth no longer serves the collective good, we will develop new economic frameworks that allocate resources in ways that enhance quality of life around the world without destroying the biosphere. If we need stronger global governance systems to tackle global issues, or enhanced localized networks to address regional resilience, they will emerge so that we can act effectively. If today's open-source, crowdfunding, and sharing-economy experiments continue to prove their worth, business-as-usual will change. Global awareness and deeper collaborative relationships among nations lead to new, shared priorities that put an end to war and poverty. Ultimately, it becomes possible to live an abundant, meaningful life within a society that restores and maintains the environment.

～

So there we have it: four distinct stories about the future that are derived from looking at our current situation and envisioning ways that multiple variables may interact and unfold. We cannot possibly know which of these will dominate the next decade—or century. Therefore, as investors needing to make decisions about an uncertain future, we must at some level *be prepared for all of them.*

Immersing ourselves in these various scenarios is one of the best ways we know to do this preparation. Cascio says that futurism (using scenarios to explore possible futures)[7] can be compared to a vaccination: "It is not a way to know what *is* going to happen but to prepare yourself for what *might* happen." As a vaccination trains your body to ward off pathogens, he says, foresight sensitizes us to changes in our world that we might not have noticed: "We suddenly start paying attention to the world in a different way because we are focused not just on what is happening now but on how what happens now evolves and emerges into the next generation."[8]

As you consider these scenarios, it may be hard to imagine today's global systems actually breaking down—or being fundamentally transformed for the better. Widespread systemic change seems almost unfathomable. As Margaret Thatcher famously said, "There is no alternative" to market capitalism as we know it. In the minds of many, the systems that govern our world today are the crowning achievement of human civilization and will serve us well into the foreseeable future. But others are not so sure, and one of the reasons why we wrote this book was to make sure that investors were at least considering this possibility.

A simple way to think about the four global scenarios might be summed up with these two questions:

- Do you think it is likely or unlikely that there will be some version of systemic change within the time frame of the investments you are considering?

- Will society respond in a coherent way? In other words, will the direction of change be positive or negative?

For example, if you think it is likely that there will be systemic change and the direction of change will be positive, that describes our breakthrough/rational emergence scenario.

Of course, as we have learned, resilient investing does *not* require you to know the answers to these monumental questions. It only asks that you consider them from time to time, take a current pulse on your outlook, and assign some probabilities. Doing so will maintain your RIM as a reliable guide even as the world continues to change.

Remember too that while any of these global scenarios is possible, that does *not* mean they are all equally likely. Each of us needs to come to our own determination about how we see the future unfolding and then take that into consideration as we make resilient investment decisions. Look at each one with as much unbiased openness as you can muster so that your resilient investing plan is drawing from all the clues that are out there on the winds.

If you accept the premise that we have been muddling along for some time, it is likely you'll conclude that this will continue for at least the foreseeable future. Yet even there, muddling through down and muddling through up are very different pictures requiring significantly different responses. Even those with faith in the long-term strength of the current system may want to be poised to respond constructively if it begins to fragment or to transform.

And consider breakdown: you do not want to be so reluctant to even give it room to exist as an option that you become an ostrich about systemic risks, nor should you let a profound despair about the future paralyze you. Similarly with breakthrough: you do not want knee-jerk cynicism to limit your ability to be part of constructive and potentially rewarding choices, and neither should profound hopes for a better future spur you to put all your chips on it. Too many things have to go right, and human dynamics may not evolve that quickly. Keeping a foot in the world as it is will balance your efforts to move things forward.

Hollywood Futures

To help make these scenarios come alive, we sometimes like to use well-known movies to dramatize what they might look like. At the breakdown/long emergency end of the spectrum is the *Mad Max* future: post-apocalyptic, global-scale economic and ecological collapse, roving bands of mutant beasts and madmen, and oil being hoarded and killed for. At the breakthrough/rational emergence end of the spectrum is the *Star Trek* world: all energy problems are solved; earth is free of conflict, money, and poverty; we've figured out what whales are all about; and we have cool gadgets like transporters, holodecks, and communicators (hey, check it out: we've already got communicators!).

Between these wild extremes are the futures that more closely resemble the world we live in now. The muddle-through-down/relentless struggle future is the *Blade Runner* scenario: not total collapse, but elites are in control, with social isolation and climate change shaping the world (it's raining all the time in Los Angeles).

Interestingly—and troublingly, once it became clear—we cannot really come up with any popular movies that sketch out a plausible muddle-through-up/incremental progress path; and indeed even our breakthrough example, *Star Trek,* doesn't give much of a clue about how we got from the heart of the Cold War to Captain Kirk. Currently, the entertainment world is raking it in by peddling apocalyptic horrors, but there are some uplifting writers. Kim Stanley Robinson believes that we need to think about a post-capitalist, utopian world; he tries to "envision things going right, and then to figure out what we could do now to put us on that course."[9] So to our readers in Hollywood: it's time to roll out some inspiring paths forward, folks!

Living with Scenarios: Staying Open to the Future

We all know how easy it is to be influenced by the latest article or news story that catches us, as well as by talking to friends who suppose they know with certainty where we are headed. When you hear someone predicting that the Dow is heading for 30,000, well, there's a muddle-through-up proponent! Gnashing of teeth, breakdown! Of course these are extremes, but with practice you will notice the worldview that lies behind *any* strongly worded opinion about the future. The key is to simply let everyone have their own ideas without reacting or trying to change them, consider what they are saying, and then make your own independent assessments.

You are likely to find voices for a spectrum even wider than the one we've presented. Someone might point you to Guy McPherson, who presents a sober argument for how climate change is likely to bring about the near-term extinction of the human race—within the next generation or two.[10] (Ouch!) At the other end is Ray Kurzweil's "singularity"; he urges us to take good care of ourselves because shortly we will have the technologies in place that could make us essentially immortal.[11] (Not sure if that's such a good idea.)

This is where we need to draw on the inner qualities of resilience that began this chapter. It takes vigilance to question the thinking of others and humility to question our own thinking, knowing that the world is a complex and dynamic place. It also bears repeating that the future is unlikely to settle into any one of these scenarios. William Gibson's line comes to mind: "The future is already here—it's just not very evenly distributed."[12]

As promised, this chapter touched on some deeply personal, interior dimensions; plunged into dystopian nightmares; and soared out to futuristic longings. How was the ride? Remember in the introduction when we said that there are no easy formulas that will help you navigate the future, to be ready for anything? The times we live in, not to mention the future that awaits, are beyond "interesting"; they are downright incredible. So let's put these perspectives and tools to work as you start to fill in the blanks of your own RIM.

CHAPTER 7

Dancing with the Future

Resilient Investor Profiles:
What Is Your D-Type?

CHAPTER 6 OPENED SOME PRETTY BIG WINDOWS, LOOKING BOTH inward and outward. With a view in each direction, the panorama invites you into the vast potential and freedom that resilient investing offers. You can see how to embrace the qualities of the martial artist, gracefully moving across the landscape of our future, engaging its unlimited potential, and aware of its unprecedented challenges.

In this chapter we see how your assessment of future scenarios helps shape the ways you direct your investments across the RIM. We will have a bit of fun with this, introducing some characters that represent various perspectives on the scenarios. They provide a playful and practical way to ensure that your resilient investing plan reflects your best thinking about what the future will ask of us. You will undoubtedly see some of yourself in one or more of these archetypes, and you'll draw on the insights you find here when you design your new RIM in chapter 8.

While these examples illustrate a range of opinions and feelings about how to be in the world and best face its future prospects, we recognize that there is a common thread that unites people of all worldviews: we all try to be diligent and discerning about the choices we have before us. Therefore we are honoring this human commonality by defining our distinctions with descriptions that start with the letter *D!*

The D-Types Guide to Future Forecasting

Most of the D-dudes and D-dames you are about to meet hold a mixed view of the future, though, as you will see, several have an abiding faith in one particular scenario. In these narratives you will see that each D-type's view of the future—his or her weighting of the scenarios' likelihoods—leads to a generalized curve that illustrates the respective forecast; and each D-type is likely to use a distinctive mix of the three investment strategies introduced in chapter 3.

We suggest that you *consider connecting your selection of investment strategies (the columns in the RIM) with your assessment of the future.* For example, if you rank breakthrough as having a significant probability, it is likely that you will want to devote a proportionate amount of your eggs to the evolutionary strategy. If you think breakdown is on the horizon, you might not want to have everything invested in the global economy. And if, like most of us, you are uncertain just where we are headed, you will want to be prepared for more than one scenario.

Without further ado, let's meet our merry band of investment caricatures! We start with three fairly straightforward ones, each of whom is closely tied to a single scenario: the Doomer, the Dreamer, and the Dealer.

The Doomer

The Doomer is convinced that we have already overstretched the earth's resources and distorted social equity to the point that environmental and socioeconomic breakdown is inevitable. **SEE FIGURE 5** Some are hunkering down to survive in a dystopian wasteland, while others are looking for constructive ways to prepare for a postindustrial world, trying to create a soft landing by working together to make it happen. Either way their primary investments are made according to the close-to-home strategy, with survivalists focusing more on personal and tangible assets and skills, and soft-landers putting significant energy into community and regional resilience.

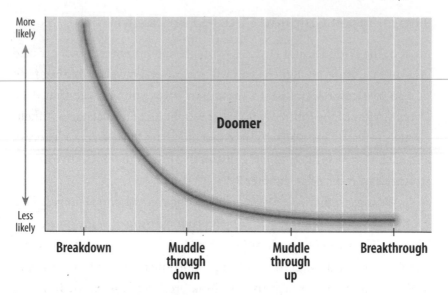

Figure 5   *The Doomer Curve*

Some will move all of their money out of the global economy column; others may keep a foot in that world, ready to divest when things really start to crumble. There will be little focus on the evolutionary column, as the emphasis is more on hunkering down with their guns, solar panels, and food or on reviving preindustrial rhythms of local self-sufficiency. Still, a few of those who have concluded that we are doomed will continue to put energy into evolutionary initiatives, including personal growth, ecosystem regeneration, and new forms of currency and exchange.

The Dreamer

The Dreamer has great faith in humanity's evolutionary destiny and is eager to be in the vanguard of the change he or she wants to see in the world. **SEE FIGURE 6** Not surprisingly, most of a Dreamer's investing energy is directed toward the evolutionary strategy, with a significant secondary focus on building healthy and sustainable homes and communities. For

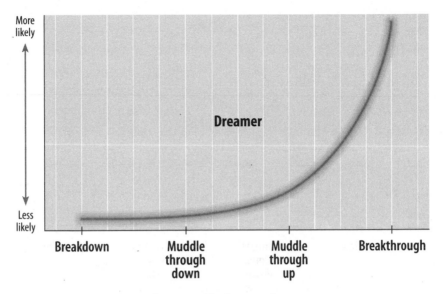

Figure 6   *The Dreamer Curve*

many Dreamers there is little purpose in remaining invested in the global economy, which seems devoid of dreams; though as with Doomers, there is a place for limited engagement in areas of the global economy where they feel they can make a difference, including personal buying and lifestyle decisions.

The Dealer

The Dealer buys heavily into the muddle-through scenarios, as he foresees that the system as it is will continue to hold together through thick and thin. SEE FIGURE 7 Dealers are aware of all of our challenges and are doing their best to "just deal with it," trying to make things better. They will often seek out investment options that are more in line with a muddle-through-up scenario, emphasizing investment in a sustainable global economy strategy while leaning away from investments and personal choices with negative social or environmental consequences.

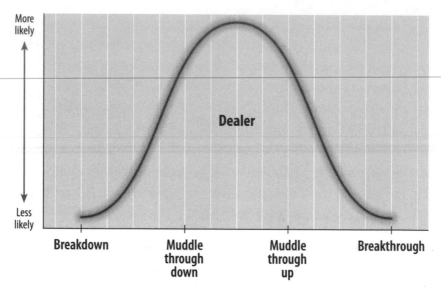

Figure 7   *The Dealer Curve*

Dealers slightly hedge their bets because they recognize that our current trajectory is uncertain. They may put a bit into forward-looking breakthrough efforts and some toward local and personal resilience that provides a buffer against modest systemic upsets or possible breakdown scenarios.

Now we turn to a couple of interesting blends: the Dualist and the Driver.

The Dualist

The Dualist is pretty sure we cannot keep going the way we have been and can easily see the potential for either breakdown or breakthrough. **SEE FIGURE 8** Some Dualists are simply of two minds: either we will break the world that we have known or we will create an amazing ecosensitive civilization. Other Dualists suggest that we will veer toward the ditch of breakdown but that the shock of that will spur great creative energy and a marshaling of economic resources that spur a subsequent breakthrough.

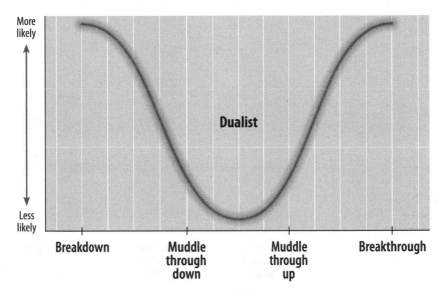

Figure 8   *The Dualist Curve*

Both types of Dualists will be heavily invested in close-to-home and evolutionary strategies (with recognition that close-to-home is beneficial for either of the Dualist visions), while their participation in the global economy will vary depending on their job and life circumstances, with investments focused on green technologies and necessary tangible goods.

The Driver

The Driver is an eco-techno-optimist. SEE FIGURE 9 Drivers see the dangers on the road ahead but say we just have to drive the car with more care and foresight. To paraphrase one of the seminal Drivers, Stewart Brand, we are at the wheel and might as well get good at it. Drivers put a lot of juice into new technology and renewable energy, both in their homes and by investing in leading-edge companies. They also emphasize the evolutionary strategy, especially social networking and building global community.

∽

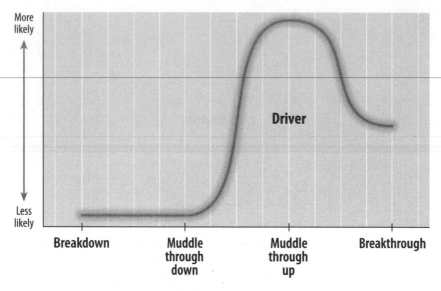

More
likely

Less
likely

Driver

Breakdown   **Muddle**   **Muddle**   **Breakthrough**
                       through   **through**
                       down   **up**

Figure 9   *The Driver Curve*

The D-types we have introduced here are just some of the more common or obvious archetypes; look around and you are likely discover a dramatic diversity of dames and dudes: the Doer, activists short on cash but rich with personal/social passion and drive; the Dawdler, who has good intentions but does not get around to implementing them; the Depleter, stubbornly insisting that the blind pursuit of private benefit is entirely justified; the Denier, who insists the global economy and environment are fine and has full faith in business-as-usual to carry us forward; the Defender, of the earth or social justice; and the Dynamo, a catalyst for spurring people's time, attention, and money into new arenas.

What Is Your D-Type?

So, who are you? Does one of our D-types strike close to home, or do you see yourself standing somewhere else in this community of resilient investors? As entertaining as our little archetypal survey may be, these past few pages are actually meant to prod your thinking and open some new windows of self-perception.

Consider:

- How much credence do you give to each of the scenarios we sketched out in chapter 6?

- How confident are you in that assessment? Do you have strong feelings, or are you more undecided?

- Does one particular scenario stand out as the most solid and prudent foundation for your resilient investing plan? If so, how much do you want to hedge your bets by preparing for the other scenarios?

- If you are giving serious consideration to either breakdown or breakthrough, what sort of time range do you envision for there to be a decisive break from our current muddling ways? One year? Twenty years?

These are substantial questions, so take some time to reflect on them; the answers will shape your resilient investing plan for years to come. Your first thoughts tell you one thing; returning to the questions after a few days or weeks may reveal new answers or directions.

The D's Go Dancing

Before we turn to helping you develop your resilient investing plan, there is one more essential element that needs to be woven into your self-assessment. You may have noticed that our D-types—including the one you most identify with—each have a fairly solid picture of the future and of their "ideal" mix of strategies. Yet by that very quality, they are falling short of the promise of our system: The resilient investor is supposed to be "ready for anything!" Yet each of our D-dudes has neglected some pieces of the puzzle. Yes, indeed, we have left our dude of all dudes,

Mr. Versatility, for the end; here he comes now, along with the dame of dames, Ms. Adaptability. Ladies and gentlemen, we are pleased to introduce you to the Dancers!

The Dancers

The Dancers embody the spirit of the martial artist you met in chapter 6: eyes soft and clear, feet light, at home in each and every one of the nine zones of the RIM. This does not mean Dancers have their assets allocated evenly among all nine zones—that would be just as rigid as being devoted to a single strategy or to *any* unchanging allocation pattern. Dancers nearly always have some degree of investment in every zone, though the weighting they use will be shaped by their worldview, just as with all the other D-types. Indeed any of the D-types we have introduced can become Dancers: just broaden your horizon a bit and you too can be a Dancing Driver or a Dualist Dancer.

Whatever D-type you may be, the final question we encourage any budding resilient investor to ask is: *How can I become more of a Dancer?* Dancers always remember that whatever their assessment of the future may be—and however they see each scenario's likelihood—the world is indeed in flux, and they need to remain poised to shift their weight and promenade a few steps in a new direction when the music slows, their children or partners in life have new needs, or the ground beneath them shifts a bit.

Good Dancers will review their investments of both time *and* money once a year or so; and they make sure that they have clarified how they will assess the returns they are getting on their personal and tangible assets (we offer some tips in chapter 8). They may shuffle time and money among various activities within many of the zones to get familiar with the full range of options at their disposal, and by so doing they become more experienced in making their allocation decisions as the years go by.

As their lives unfold, the areas of the RIM that Dancers prioritize for new and additional investment shift as conditions change:

- The global situation and opportunities

- Their personal financial situation

- The stages of their life

- The evolution of their own particular passions and capacities over the course of their life

As you design your own resilient investing plan, be sure to consider what you might add to your initial D-type mix that would help you become a better Dancer. The specific changes will be very individualized; you should target areas of growth that complement what you are already doing, adding to your long-term responsiveness and resilience. Maybe you are a good waltzer, but is it time to tango? Learning new steps means you will be ready when the music changes.

Now, having gained some deeper perspectives on resiliency and our future in chapter 6 and with your newly discovered D-identity in hand, it is time to roll up your sleeves and start designing a fresh, new version of your RIM that reflects all you have learned and all you hope to create in your life.

CHAPTER 8

Your Resilient Investing Plan

Designing, Implementing, and Evaluating
Your Resilient Investing Plan

WE HAVE COME A LONG WAY TOGETHER, AND YOU'VE BUILT UP A clear understanding of the resilient investing landscape—the new framework of the RIM along with your own worldview and priorities. You are indeed ready to face the uncertainty of tomorrow by having a future-proof portfolio in hand. Now it's time for the rubber to meet the road.

There are many kinds of travelers. Whether you do comprehensive research and decision making on your own, or tend to collaborate with professionals, or follow an inner compass that points you toward your next destination, we want to help you find a path that will enhance your life while making the world a better place. However you make your decisions, you will want to do all you can to ensure that your choices fully reflect your sense of purpose and long-term goals.

In the pages that follow, we outline a step-by-step process that will help you map your route forward. Of course this is just the skeleton of how it would look in practice—the flesh and blood come from your own reflections and conversations. Whether you follow the structure we lay out here or take a different approach to the process of personal change, you will want to carry these questions with you—to a personal retreat, in conversation with loved ones, on long quiet hikes, or as part of your consultations with trusted advisors. As you do, you are likely to find that the resilient perspective has become integrated into the ways you process new experiences and contemplate the future.

The Power of the Planning Retreat

Making time for careful planning and diligent assessment is not easy; it requires prior thought, commitment, follow-through, and sometimes considerable negotiation with bosses and spouses. But we highly recommend that you plan to take some time away to, uh, plan—we call this the "plan to plan" rule. Cue the planning retreat. It may be a single day or, even better, a weekend that includes periods of diligent thinking, physical activity, and time for quiet reflection.

A periodic retreat is a great tool to facilitate personal growth and make progress on your resilient investing plan; Christopher, one of the authors, aims for at least one a year. Our experience has shown that taking time away from the daily frenzy of life to pause and reflect on progress and challenges brings renewed vigor and enhanced vision to a life well lived. If you want to keep your dance steps fresh, it is an invaluable investment.

STEP 1

Visioning: Where Do You Want to Go?

In chapter 5 you created an initial picture of how you are investing across the Resilient Investing Map, noting your specific investments zone by zone. You have also dug a little deeper and identified which assets are most important, and available, to you. Now the question is: *Where do you want to go?* Recall this definition from the beginning of this book: *investing is something that we all do by directing our time, attention, energy, or money in ways that move us toward our future dreams, using a diverse range of strategies.*

It's time to envision those future dreams and rise up to your full Dancing Diva potential. You have probably been intrigued by a few of the things we mentioned in the previous chapters that you haven't yet been involved in; and perhaps you have remembered things that you've done at some point in the past but are not doing right now.

Looking at where you fall on the spectrum of worldviews about our future has probably generated a bunch more ways to make tweaks and changes. If you see yourself as a Dreamer but you are living like a Dawdler, naturally that suggests a shift in focus. Or maybe you've been dealing with it more than you would like; where do you want to take more control of setting your direction? And whatever D you may be, what does the future you see suggest about the mix of strategies you'd like to be involved in as you go forward? For example, if you give the breakdown scenario a high probability, wouldn't it make sense to have a solid chunk of your investments close to home? Visit the book's website to complete an online self-assessment that will get you started.

Mostly, it is important to take some time to reflect on the bigger picture of your life. Consider where you would like to see yourself in five years and 10 years. How would you like your life to unfold or change or improve? Think big here! These are the types of questions best pondered over a few weeks. Being outdoors helps, too; a long hike or a weekend at the beach are perfect opportunities to sink into this broader and deeper inquiry. How can you take the self-assessment you did in chapter 5, including your first glimmers of what it will take to become more of a Dancer, and infuse it with this forward-looking visioning?

STEP 2

Explore Your Options

It's time to turn your attention to specifics: what actions can you take to move from where you are to where you'd like to be? At this stage it's best to cast your gaze wide and consider a full range of possibilities. After you gather a large number of good investment ideas, you'll zero in on the most valuable and doable next steps.

So, now that the RIM is modifying how you look at your time and money, what new possibilities or changes have popped up? Do you see one or several areas on your map where you clearly want to do more, whether particular zones or entire rows or columns? Alternatively, are there areas that you've been overemphasizing? Jot down anything that you may want to consider adding to each zone in the months or years to come; be as specific or general as you like. Of course, remember that the book's website has updated ideas and opportunities for each of the nine zones.

In our experience the challenge usually is not finding new ideas—it is winnowing down a hefty pile and filtering the possibilities based on relevance, timeliness, and priority. Many of us feel even more constrained with our time than with our money, given commitments to work and family. Ask yourself, *What can I let go of to make room for this?* Even if you are excited about your new directions, overextending yourself—your time or money—is never sustainable. Remember that this process is meant to increase your true wealth, so don't neglect those closest to you, your physical health, or your professional life—keep an eye on all the zones of your map, not just your areas of new focus.

One simple tool that we have found particularly helpful for brainstorming, tracking, and prioritizing a pile of ideas is to use 3 × 5 cards. It is low tech, but it works, especially when you have a lot of new ideas, directions, and life-hacks to consider. Choose the best of the ideas you've collected so far; some may require more than one action-item card. Include the most relevant key information on each card: name or title (what are you calling this idea?), what zone it is relevant to, estimated cost, estimated return (if you can determine), brief description of its purpose, estimated time to completion (days, weeks, years), and other cards that relate to a shared goal. Figure 10 shows how Dan the Dealer, a character we will meet in a moment, might fill out a card for one of his zone 1 investments. **SEE FIGURE 10**

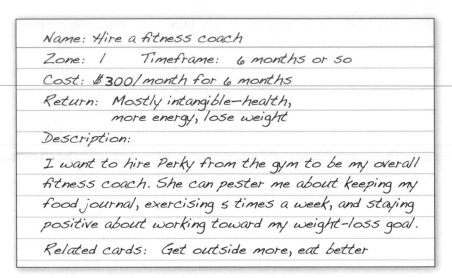

Name: Hire a fitness coach
Zone: 1   Timeframe: 6 months or so
Cost: $300/month for 6 months
Return: Mostly intangible—health,
            more energy, lose weight
Description:

I want to hire Perky from the gym to be my overall
fitness coach. She can pester me about keeping my
food journal, exercising 5 times a week, and staying
positive about working toward my weight-loss goal.
Related cards: Get outside more, eat better

Figure 10   *Example of a 3" × 5" Idea Card*

Create a 3 × 5 card for each idea; you can work on this in your spare time for a few days or weeks. One nice thing about the cards is that you can fan them out on a table, grouping by zone, column, or row, and experiment with prioritizing and seeing how they work together. After you have played with your cards for a while, it's time to start making some decisions. Do some further meaningful pruning to bring your list down to a collection of fewer than 10 new goals or opportunities; drop the wacky and promote the wonderful. The top ideas get promoted to the next phase, but keep the other cards; in a year or two, you will want to look back and review them for possible future inclusion.

STEP 3

Prioritize Your Options

Next we select our best ideas and see how we can work them together, including laying out an achievable sequence of steps. The preliminary work can be done in smaller snippets of time, but from here on out you will want to make time for in-depth reflection. Once the designated moment arrives, find a spot outside or by a window with a lovely view, and, if you like, grab a cup of your preferred form of caffeination.

Is there an idea that is jumping up and down with its hand up, just looking for you to call on it? If so, bingo, that's probably what you should consider first. Looking ahead a year or two, does anything pop out as a natural next step? Perhaps your life is already so well tuned that you need only small adjustments to a couple of zones to help everything sing; see how you can give those areas a nudge. Can you put some things in place right away that will create opportunities for new investments in the following year? Maybe you need to take care of some mundane issues (new roof for the house) before moving on to ideas that truly inspire you. Thinking ahead, are there ideas that would work in three to five years? Seeds that you plant now can germinate and sprout as you find ways to allocate more time, attention, or money to them. Some of your ideas may seem a bit far afield, but with a little skill and luck you could coax them to take root and reap an abundant harvest.

Now that you have oriented yourself, let's take the process a little further. Consider the following criteria as you continue to organize and prioritize. You do not need to address every one of these considerations; hold them lightly and follow the threads that feel most relevant to your situation.

Time

Which aspects of your schedule can shift to make room for new initiatives? Some actions are as quick as a phone call; others take weeks or years to come to fruition. Balance the time you have available and the level of sustained attention you can give with the demands of the new opportunities you are considering.

Money

What will each new action or investment idea cost? Can you sketch out a budget (rough or precise)? How is your overall budget, and what level of financial burden can you accept? Can you save first before proceeding, or does it make sense to borrow money to make it happen? Could you consider sharing the cost and the resource with others? How about bartering for what you want? Can you reallocate resources from other zones; for example, can you sell some mutual funds to pay for home upgrades?

Return on Investment

Evaluating returns can be a complex project, even for investment advisors! Can you estimate your future income or savings from the new investment ideas you're considering? Even a rough sketch of returns is helpful (see "Evaluating Nonfinancial Returns" in chapter 5 and Resource 2: The Investor's Eye at the back of the book).

Personal Skills and Level of Support

Can you implement your choices? If not, can you learn or partner with someone who is skilled? What resources are available that can improve the chances of success? Do you have family members or friends who might be willing to share the work and learn alongside you, such as a buddy with construction skills that complement your own? If you have access to low-interest loans from family or friends, this will obviously make additional investment strategies available to you. What about online community support? Check for individuals, organizations, and businesses that may be a good fit for collaboration.

Professional Assistance

Hiring professionals is another important area for consideration. Even if you are frugal by nature or necessity, it can often be cost-effective to hire expertise rather than try to learn everything yourself. Competent coaching and support can often mean the difference between success and failure.

Now that you have looked a little deeper, done some nipping and tucking of ideas, and settled on your priorities, you are ready to start bringing your new ideas to life—let's dance!

Sequencing: Choreograph Your Dance

Your choreography will lay out the first few action steps, say, over the first six months, then another objective or two in the next year or so, and then any additional projects to be activated over the next three to five years. You can always improvise around whatever structure you lay out, but having a basic framework will help you keep the big picture in mind. Stack those 3 × 5 cards in order or just make a list. Rough out your dollar estimates next to the ideas or note if you need to do a little more research; likewise consider the time commitments for each and whether the demands on your time will be regular or episodic. Double-check that the way you have laid things out makes sense; relying on this master action-item list will keep you on track.

Now is the time to begin drafting your new RIM; transfer your current and new ideas onto a fresh map and see how it all fits together. To see how that looks in practice, let's take a look at a couple of examples. We will meet Dan, who filled out the 3 × 5 card in figure 10, and also check in on Dahlia and Adele, whose first-round RIMs we saw in chapter 5. The following RIM examples include just their new activity; you may want to create a more complete map that includes all of your existing and new investments.

Dan the Dealer

Through exposure to the RIM, Dan the Dealer, who has a 9-to-5 sales job, realizes that he has been concerned about the state of the world (and his life) and decides to become more self-sufficient and connected to his home community. **SEE FIGURE 11** Here is his sequence of implementation for the next couple of years:

- Immediately: start saving 20 percent of his net income, invested in a blend of SRI mutual funds that hold both bonds and stocks (zone 8)

- Six months: scale back sales travel (zone 2); join a couple of community groups (Rotary? Transition town?) (zone 1); plant a garden in the backyard (zone 4)

- One year: investigate a more local occupation and career (zones 1 and 2); lose 25 pounds by exercising and hiking more with his son (zone 1)

- Three years: investigate buying a smaller house with enough land to grow food (zone 4)

| THREE CORE INVESTMENT STRATEGIES | | |
Close to Home	Sustainable Global Economy	Evolutionary
1 Join community service groups (Rotary?) Research a locally based career Exercise and hike more!	**2** – – Reduce work travel	**3** + Take some gardening classes
4 + Plant a vegetable garden Look for a smaller house with gardens	**5** – – Avoid overshopping and save money	**6** (No new activity)
7 + Build emergency fund at local credit union	**8** + + Save 20% of income Invest in SRI funds	**9** (No new activity)

(Row labels at left: Personal/Social, Tangible, Financial. Vertical axis label: THREE KINDS OF ASSETS/TYPES OF RETURN)

Figure 11   *Dan the Dealer's Mixed RIM*

Dahlia the Driver

Dahlia the Driver's top priority is pushing herself at work to learn quickly and improve her career prospects. **SEE FIGURE 12** She's also attending a local Toastmasters group, improving her presentation skills, and volunteering (for now) as a blog editor to help build and diversify her skills. Paying off her college loans is her second most important goal over the next couple of years, and she is limiting her zone 5 purchases to help improve her financial situation.

	THREE CORE INVESTMENT STRATEGIES		
	Close to Home	**Sustainable Global Economy**	**Evolutionary**
Personal/ Social	**1** ++ Toastmasters for presentation skills Healthy	**2** ++ Just starting career, working with mentor Blog editor on the side	**3** Yoga DVDs Backpacking trips with friends
Tangible	**4** (No new activity)	**5** Defer/minimize/ live simply	**6** (No new activity)
Financial	**7** Minimal savings in local bank	**8** Paying off college loans quickly	**9** (No new activity)

(Left vertical axis label: THREE KINDS OF ASSETS / TYPES OF RETURN)

Figure 12   *Dahlia the Driver's Dancing RIM*

Adele Adaptability

Adele Adaptability is a Dreamer who now realizes that she wants to become more of a Dancing Dreamer. SEE FIGURE 13 During her RIM inventory, she noted that her house could be more energy efficient (zone 4) and that although her backyard has lots of sun, it has mostly been taken over by roses and dandelions. The big burr under her saddle is her job: she is making good money, but she is not very inspired by her career (zone 2).

As soon as she started filling in the RIM, her home and livelihood really popped out at her. Her first investment will be an energy audit for her house—and she is committed to spending a few thousand dollars to

	THREE CORE INVESTMENT STRATEGIES		
	Close to Home	Sustainable Global Economy	Evolutionary
Personal/ Social	**1** Maintain and sustain Personal retreat time to stay on track	**2** – Research new career and start moving into it	**3** – – Fewer conferences Redirect time and assets to career search and home improvements
Tangible	**4** + + Renewable energy and energy efficiency upgrades to house Fabulous edible gardens!	**5** (No new activity)	**6** (No new activity)
Financial	**7** (No new activity)	**8** (No new activity)	**9** (No new activity)

THREE KINDS OF ASSETS / TYPES OF RETURN

Figure 13   *Adele the Dreamer's Dancing RIM*

improve whatever problems the audit uncovers. She is going to talk with a career consultant to begin the process of realigning her career with her Dreamer aspirations and has scheduled a resilient investor planning retreat to keep herself on track.

Her sequence might look something like this:

- Six months: energy audit and appointment with career counselor

- One year: do basic energy efficiency upgrades to the house and work on some of the things the career counselor suggested

- One to two years: attend one fewer personal growth workshops (for a savings of $1,000) to redirect capital and time into developing career options

- Three years: move into a new job and plant the backyard with fruit trees and planter boxes for tomatoes and lettuce

Are you beginning to see some possible paths of your own? What can *you* do in the next six months, year, and three years? What can you *stop* doing—to free up time, attention, and possibly cash—to fuel your next steps? As you move toward completion of the design phase, make dates with yourself to periodically return your attention and focus to fine-tuning your plan.

STEP 5
Stepping Out: It's Time to Dance!

Now that you have crafted a solid and resilient plan of action, it's time to step onto that shiny dance floor! We have four core suggestions that are relevant for almost anyone implementing ambitious new plans.

- For any new endeavor, *start small* to help limit risk and improve the chances of success. When you are learning, don't take too big of a bite so that you make the inevitable errors with fewer dollars or less time at risk. We like using *small-scale trials* to test new ideas and activities.

- We strongly urge people to *schedule tasks,* especially anything that is new or outside your normal routine. When you are at the end of the planning process, make a point to add next steps to your calendar, and don't be afraid to set deadlines.

- The relative speed and perseverance of tortoises and hares aside, there is not much argument against *slow and steady* being the mantra for long-term goal accomplishment. Racing around and forcing more urgency into life is no fun, and it's not sustainable.

- And remember that the goal here isn't just productivity and task accomplishment; cycle through again and dare to dream big! The actual phrase we use is *dream big, start small,* which reflects a lovely practical-visionary combination. If you are considering a bigger transformation, such as changing your career or moving to a new town or property, give yourself plenty of time to prepare.

If you are challenging yourself as we hope you are, there will be some steps you've slotted into your choreography that are new to you. One of the great benefits of the Internet age is the ubiquity of information; it is easy to learn how to do almost anything! Make use of this free guidance, but be sure to confirm how reliable and experienced the sources are.[1]

STEP 6
Dancing till Dawn: Evaluate, Modify, Repeat

The final step of the design process is to keep on dancing! Central to the *resilient* part of being a resilient investor is a process of evaluation and tweaking of your plan as the years go by. Periodically, you will want to look back at how your plan performed and take a fresh tour through all these steps as you adapt your plan for its next stage.

How has the past year been? Overall, what has gone well? Were there challenges? More specifically, how did the new investments or ideas that you implemented in the past year turn out? Successes? Failures? Are there things that are on track as is or that could use a slight nudge?

What should be discontinued? Review your plan or plans from previous years: what had you set out for yourself to be working on in the coming year or two? Take some time to sit comfortably, contemplate and reflect, and take notes.

You will want to devote time and focus to evaluate both successful investments and those that haven't turned out as planned. Perhaps some new ideas or investment opportunities have become available that you can now include. Has your view of the world—and the future—shifted? Maybe you now identify with a different D-type or your availability of time and money has changed. Modify your plan or create something completely new: it's your life; make it what you want!

Every journey begins with a single step, and now you are well along the road you have chosen. You've learned how to see your life through this expanded view of investing and embraced the goal of becoming increasingly resilient as the years go by. Make a celebratory list of everything that has moved forward since your previous planning session—and put it on your wall to remind you that each day is a chance to dance your way toward your dreams.

CHAPTER 9

Tales of Resilient Living

The Authors' Stories

Now that you have learned to dance and designed your RIM, perhaps your head is spinning as you consider the multitude of destinations that you could choose to visit. We have asked you to do some challenging work, but now you can put away your colored pencils and sketches. This chapter offers a change of pace and provides a more personal perspective on the journey.

Travelers have always gathered together, around watering holes and in roadhouses, to unwind, share stories, and tell tales. Swapping travel guides and poring over tattered maps is half the fun of it all! More importantly, it helps us remember that *the map is not the territory; even a big map can convey only a fraction of what you will find once you get started.

In this spirit, here are three snippets about how we are personally using the Resilient Investing Map. Of course we don't hold ourselves up as role models; each of us has banged his head against many hard objects, juggled too many balls in the name of wanting it all, or found his own bad habits getting him into trouble. And we are not the most diverse collection—three college-educated white guys who all co-own a specialty investment company. Yet we've earned our gray hairs by practicing what we preach, particularly in the investment realm; we hope that our experience and expertise offer some lessons that have value to others.

So make yourself comfortable, and the Natural Dudes will regale you with some highlights from our travels. As you will see, we all use the RIM differently, and each shares his tale in his own distinct voice and style.

Hal Brill: Dilemmas of a Dualist

It ain't easy being a Dualist! We lack faith in the status quo but are uncertain about what might replace it. Some days I'm optimistic that the long trajectory of civilization will continue on its arc of development, with new technologies in the service of evolving human consciousness bringing us into a breakthrough future. Other times I'm dejected, seeing that we are destroying the biosphere and mired in economic and social quicksand. This is my Dualist cross to bear, and I know I'm not alone, so let me tell you how I've lightened its load.

I was raised with a great love of nature, so it was fitting that my first jobs were in outdoor education. But I was keenly aware that my students would forget what they learned as soon as they returned to their suburbs and cities, places that to me symbolized man's separation from nature. I felt that society as a whole needed to change, but I did not know what I could do about it.

So I traveled, including a pilgrimage with a group called Walk for the Earth, crossing the United States and Europe. Later, in remote Middle-Eastern villages, I saw Coca-Cola signs and TV antennas beaming in Western consumer values. All of this reaffirmed my commitment to activism in my home country. Now, using the RIM, I can see that I was investing my time and energy (I didn't have extra money) into zones 1 and 2.

On my thirtieth birthday, I moved to Santa Fe, New Mexico, where I helped launch several organizations. My passion was to start an "eco-village," demonstrating how to sustainably meet human needs (zones 3 and 6). I participated in community finance, as it was necessary to raise capital to make this dream a reality (zone 7). Many of the ecological design principles we promoted worked their way into the mainstream (zone 6). But I also learned some painful lessons, as our band of visionaries fell short on our dream of creating the model village.

Next I helped my father, Jack Brill, research his book *Investing from the Heart: The Guide to Socially Responsible Investments and Money Management*, and we soon founded Natural Investments. Paul Hawken's *The Ecology of Commerce: A Declaration of Sustainability* strongly influenced me, as it clarified the importance of mobilizing corporations to address the spiraling ecological crisis (zone 8). Knowing that capital could be a potent leverage point, I decided to become a financial advisor so that I could help investors shift their money.

But as a Dualist, this choice felt strange. I wanted nothing to do with Wall Street! The global economy always seemed tenuous to me; I couldn't fathom how a system that depends on exponential economic growth could continue indefinitely on a finite planet. Fortunately, I found business partners who shared a vision of growing an investment company that *does* consider systemic risk and offers meaningful alternatives.

Today my resilient investing plan looks something like this.
SEE FIGURE 14

Close to Home

My wife and I designed a natural, passive solar home, and Hawks Haven, a green neighborhood in tiny Paonia, Colorado. We voraciously support our local farmers and serve on nonprofit boards. I have invested in an organic hops farm and have lent money to neighbors for their land purchases. I'm always looking for ways to enhance local and regional resilience.

Sustainable Global Economy

This has been my main livelihood focus, and my retirement money is invested using Natural Investments portfolios. We try to make our purchases as green and conscientious as possible. I would like to get an electric bicycle to help me up the hill with our farm produce and groceries.

THREE CORE INVESTMENT STRATEGIES			
THREE KINDS OF ASSETS/TYPES OF RETURN	**Close to Home**	**Sustainable Global Economy**	**Evolutionary**
Personal/ Social	**1** Community engagement Exercise	**2** Natural Investments, LLC	**3** Research Mind/body practice
Tangible	**4** Solar panels High Wire Hops farm	**5** Hybrid car Nice kitchen	**6** Conservation easements
Financial	**7** Local investments in people I know	**8** SRI retirement accounts	**9** Self-directed IRA with impact

Figure 14   *Hal Brill's RIM*

Evolutionary

This has mostly been about learning, personal growth, yoga, hiking and skiing, and playing the bass. I have protected land with conservation easements, invested in tree farms and solar projects, and have long been part of the community investing world, both through my work and as an investor. My goal is to use this book as a platform to help bring about an evolutionary future!

Most of my life has unfolded in a mostly unplanned manner; John Lennon's well-known line about life being what happens while we are busy making other plans resonates with me. I regularly spend time in nature, reflecting on my life and noticing what a long, strange trip it's been. I've never been disciplined enough to do the 3 × 5 card process in chapter 8, but I do find it exceedingly helpful to sketch out my RIM at least annually so that I can see how things have unfolded and glimpse areas for future focus.

Michael Kramer: Weaving the Dream

As a Dreamer, I am the first to embrace anything that can help raise consciousness and improve the human condition. While being aware of the structural problems and risks of civilization's trajectory, I prefer to focus on game-changing solutions and feel fortunate to have discovered the sustainable design discipline of permaculture 25 years ago. That inspiration gave me hope and spawned investments in my own learning and teaching about regenerative living (I still lead a permaculture teacher training periodically), conscious shopping and business practices, and sustainable and responsible investing. I was one of Hal's first clients in 1990 before joining the firm as an advisor in 2000.

I moved to Hawaii in 1999 as I was studying for my securities license, a decision steeped in resilient thinking. I wanted to live in a place with year-round agriculture and adequate water and also felt the need to make more money to support my family. More profoundly, I was harboring some major political and economic concerns about the future direction of the country and so wanted to have "lifestyle immunity" from mainstream America; I had every intention of moving to another country if things fell apart in the United States, so it felt like a strategic self-preservation move. As I sit here 15 years later writing this from my outdoor home office overlooking a jungle forest, it feels like one of the best decisions I ever made.

I have explored green lifestyle choices for 25 years, joining CSA farms, building a passive solar house with radiant floor heat, catching rooftop rainwater, and having vegetable gardens and fruit and nut trees. Here on Hawaii Island there is a sense of food abundance, and I can trade my homegrown produce for fish. To foster community self-reliance, I eat and buy locally as much as possible, including owning a diesel Jeep so that I can use biodiesel fuel produced from locally sourced waste oil. I am fully committed to recycling, composting, and shopping at locally owned businesses whenever possible. I even founded the island's Think Local Buy Local campaign to encourage this.

I am also working to create an eco/agricultural neighborhood on Maui that will fulfill my dream of living in community among fields and orchards of organic food, using renewable energy, and living in the greenest possible home. This seems resilient for my future food, shelter, and energy needs and will intentionally diversify and localize my income.

A great deal of my time and energy goes into being a voice for positive change through civic engagement, writing columns, and volunteerism, including my role on the national SRI policy committee and dialogue with corporate management. Local green economy and sustainability initiatives are another focus of my time. I am active at the state legislature on matters of sustainability and environmental protection, and I serve on civic commissions and nonprofit boards.

Clearly, I invest a lot of time and personal energy in pursuit of my Dreamer agenda. Meanwhile my financial assets primarily include co-owning Natural Investments and investment properties; I also have an IRA with SRI mutual funds and community development investments. These support societal resiliency and my eventual retirement, though I am aware of how tied to the global corporate economy my livelihood is.

Using the RIM to roughly quantify my overall allocations of time, attention, and money among the nine zones, I have concluded that half of my overall investments are engaged in various evolutionary strategies and that I also clearly prioritize growing my personal assets. **SEE FIGURE 15**

Being a Dreamer means I have a lot of hope for the future, and my investment allocation reflects that. I continue to work on ways to devote more attention to self-care, especially practicing yoga and playing music, and for my daily life to be more under my local control should the global

| THREE CORE INVESTMENT STRATEGIES | | | |
	Close to Home	Sustainable Global Economy	Evolutionary	Totals
Personal/ Social	**1** 15%	**2** 10%	**3** 25%	**50%**
Tangible	**4** 5%	**5** 5%	**6** 10%	**20%**
Financial	**7** 5%	**8** 10%	**9** 15%	**30%**
Totals	**25%**	**25%**	**50%**	**100%**

(Left vertical axis label: THREE KINDS OF ASSETS/TYPES OF RETURN)

Figure 15　*Michael Kramer's RIM*

corporate economy struggle in any significant way. I have other dreams to pursue in the coming years: recording an album, writing more books, public speaking, perhaps even running for elected office. Where's a cloning machine when you need one?!

Christopher Peck: Road Map of a Dancing Driver

I see myself as a Dancing Driver. If I had a tagline, it would be *I get it; there are problems. How do we solve them?* Or maybe, *Don't fight the system—replace it.* As an Eagle Scout ("Be prepared!") and lifelong designer, I love to step back and reflect on systems, evaluate options, decide, act, and persuade others to join me. From a scenario perspective, I believe we have been muddling through up for centuries; Hans Rosling's graphical representations prove it for the past 40 years,[1] and I think that will continue to be our destiny. But I learned about global warming in 1991, and I am old enough to have seen some of my woods turned into parking lots, so I'm sympathetic to breakdown concerns.

I'm inspired by Stewart Brand and Kevin Kelly and the invocation to use tools and ideas to change the world. I clearly remember sitting in the basement of the St. John's College library in Annapolis in 1987 and discovering the *Whole Earth Catalog.* I buried myself in it until the library closed, with a mixture of mind-popping delight (so many cool things in one place!) and under-the-skin frustration (why had no one shared this with me before?). Whole-systems thinking, inspired by Buckminster Fuller and Eastern philosophy, became my basis. I found permaculture in 1990, when co-founder Bill Mollison visited Santa Fe, New Mexico, and was enthralled with the comprehensive and positivistic approach.

I left Santa Fe in 1999 to come to California and build a sustainable investment business, with a 10-year plan to find a life partner, buy some land to develop a homestead, and root myself into a climate and a community with more inherent resilience than the high desert. California has its own challenges with water and well-being, but the ease of growing food here can't be beat. And the community of transformative thinkers and doers on the left coast enhances my growth and learning.

When my wife and I were looking to purchase property in Sonoma County (note the life partner and business success!), we started from a similar holistic perspective. When we told our real estate agents that we were looking for a "just right fixer-upper with good bones on more than an acre, with an east-west orientation and within walking distance of a vibrant downtown," well, they looked a little shocked. We wanted enough land so that we could grow food for our family; who knows what the future might bring. We wanted to be in town, where the Internet is fast and it is easy to bike to necessities for our growing family (our young son loves homegrown asparagus!). We wanted a house we could live in and where a deep energy retrofit made financial sense; the east-west orientation is for the solar panels. My parents now live on our property, and my wife's parents live just a couple of blocks away. All this has deepened our family and community resilience.

I have been a practicing Zen Buddhist for the past 20 years. My worldview is heavily influenced by Taoism and a connection to wilderness. I have a black belt in aikido, and I study tai chi. These practices keep me light on my feet, in the flow, responsive to whatever happens day to day, and lively enough to keep driving toward a better world.

Looking forward, I remember that I am living the dream right now, with additional investments serving to fine-tune an instrument already humming along. As a new dad, boosting personal assets is essential; I work to keep my growth practices lively and my marriage humorous. Lone Palm Ranch, our one-acre homestead, continues to develop, using less energy and growing more food every year. A model of resilient storm water management and delicious perennial plantings, our home has been the destination of garden tours in our region. We have a few more years of five-figure investments until it is fully sustaining. My ownership stake in Natural Investments will continue as my largest financial asset and thankfully a fun, right livelihood.

I am showing an abridged version of our RIM, highlighting zone by zone how I have increased, decreased, or stayed the same with my investment. You can see that I have really cranked up zone 1 (daddy time); everything else is seeing modest tunings. SEE FIGURE 16

Reflections

What might we glean from these tales? First it is clear that we have lived fairly unorthodox lives (and of course we've left out quite a bit of "color" from these brief bios!). Second, you will notice that our investments

THREE CORE INVESTMENT STRATEGIES			
	Close to Home	**Sustainable Global Economy**	**Evolutionary**
Personal/ Social	**1** **+ + + +** Daddy time	**2** Hold steady	**3** **– –** Stay home more
Tangible	**4** **+ +** Homestead keeps developing	**5** Hold steady	**6** Hold steady
Financial	**7** Hold steady	**8** **+** Continue retirement funding	**9** Hold steady

THREE KINDS OF ASSETS/TYPES OF RETURN

Figure 16   *Christopher Peck's RIM*

evolved as we moved through our lives. In our younger years, with little money, we devoted ourselves to learning skills, connecting in deep ways with nature, and participating in projects that matched our passions (some of which didn't work out as we had hoped). Later we each gravitated to the idea that money could be used as a transformative tool for societal change, and when we realized this was a shared career goal, we formed our company. And, third, we are now and always will be works in progress. We all rebalance within the RIM as needed, putting more energy into one area for a period (for example, writing this book has been a huge investment of our time into zones 2 and 3); likewise we respond to changes in the world, our family dynamics, and our own aging process—all of which inform our decisions about which zone of the RIM to focus on.

We have been making investments with our time and money for many years, striving to walk our talk and live meaningful lives. But until now we didn't have the benefit of the RIM to help us see exactly where we were putting our energies and how it all fits together. Now, at the tail end of the writing process, we can reflect on our own life experience as a way to show that this system really works. The RIM gives us a way to observe and analyze ourselves, to see exactly where on the map we are choosing to invest our time, attention, and money, and to then help us see what changes we wish to make and how to make them.

We hope these examples inspire you to do your own reflections. How would you map out the decisions that you made when you were younger? Where are you at today, and where would you like to be heading? Are you considering the full array of possible futures that awaits us as we head into the mystery?

In the end, despite our continued positing that the idea of investing needs to be expanded, there comes a time to drop the distinctions that divide our lives into categories. There is only one activity that we are all engaged with all the time: we are simply trying to live our lives the best we can. And so, although we have been calling it *resilient investing* throughout the book, our deepest wish is that this lens, and these tools, will support you on your path toward something even more enticing: *resilient living*.

CHAPTER 10

The Invisible Heart
of Resilience

How Becoming Personally Resilient
Helps Create a Resilient World

YOU MAY RECALL THAT WE MADE A RATHER BOLD CLAIM IN THE introduction, stating, "the strategies that best prepare you and your family for a range of future scenarios *are inherently beneficial to the systems upon which civilization and all life depend.*" In this final chapter, we explore the roots and the far-reaching consequences of this idea. We conclude by envisioning how a brighter future could take shape as more people begin using the lens of resilience to guide their decisions.

For those with even a cursory interest in economics, there is likely a familiar ring to the idea that pursuit of personal interests yields societal benefits. We touched on this in chapter 3 when we laid out the show me the money strategy, a values-neutral approach to asset allocation derived from Adam Smith's "invisible hand of the market." Unfortunately, it has become all too evident that a civilization based solely on competition and maximizing self-interest does not always create the desired benefits or distribute them equitably. In fact, it can frequently cause great harm to people and nature.

Nonetheless, as we have developed and worked with the RIM, we've come to appreciate the nugget of truth in Smith's teachings. What he lacked—or at least what is lacking in the way he is interpreted today—is a big enough perspective on what is meant by the pursuit of an individual's best interests. By expanding the definition of what *self-interest* really means, the essence of Smith's teachings may take on newfound relevance in a world searching for answers to complex challenges.

Here's why: In our experience, when investors broaden their goals so that they focus not solely on their financial assets but their personal and tangible ones as well, they tend to utilize strategies (such as those described in this book) that enhance the health of the community and the environment. Conversely, investments that harm the fabric of society fall out of favor because they make us less resilient. Many people realize (to take two obvious examples) that a deteriorating global environment and extreme levels of inequality are detrimental to everyone, and they understand the folly of profiting financially while furthering negative trends.

We have coined the term *invisible heart* to reflect this larger view of self-interest. It does not ignore the financial realm but recognizes that a hand left to its own devices can be used for healing or can cause harm. *A hand needs a heart to guide it.* We are all connected in more ways than we can fathom; as more people recognize this, the ancient and universal wisdom of the Golden Rule—to not harm others—becomes a foundational principle that guides our decisions.

Here is our expression of the invisible heart principle:

> When investors take a comprehensive approach to enhancing their self-interest, one that is larger than solely personal or financial, the *invisible heart of resilience* exerts a tendency to enhance societal well-being.

Throughout this book we have seen how becoming more resilient empowers individuals and prepares them for an uncertain future. Now we can appreciate that the effectiveness of these strategies is strengthened by the fact that we are also investing to support community and environmental relationships on which we all depend.

The invisible hand implies that there is no need to consciously decide to be of service—the mere fact that one is successful in the market implies that one has done something beneficial for society. But as we have seen, there are many entrepreneurs today who are deliberately combining their profit-making ambitions with their zeal to make a difference in the world. This is not just about such practices being good for business; it is about creating the societal and environmental conditions necessary for people of all economic classes to thrive. The invisible heart builds on these intentions, enabling investors to use all three of our asset types (personal, tangible, and financial) to yield larger benefits. Embracing the triple bottom line of "people, planet, and profit" is what makes true resilience possible.

For decades we and our colleagues have been urging investors to adopt this bigger perspective. Today there are ever more opportunities to strengthen communities and revitalize ecosystems. All three of the strategies that we included in the RIM (close to home, global economy, and evolutionary) were designed to bring about positive outcomes in the larger world that we inhabit. For some time each of them has been tracking upward on a slow-but-steadily-rising growth curve, and over the past decade they have all seen a surge in both popular interest and institutional adoption.

Let's imagine that this continues and even accelerates as the invisible heart unfolds its beneficence. What would our world look like if all nine baskets get filled to overflowing by enthusiastic, resilient investors?

Close-to-Home Investing: Creating Resilient Communities

In many communities all it takes to get inspired about the power of localism is to visit the weekly farmers market. Besides the fresh and delicious food, we often find local musicians, nonprofit groups, and, most of all, plenty of opportunity to bump into your neighbors and catch up on their doings. New weekly markets are popping up in ever smaller towns, while the long-established ones keep growing—in Boulder, Colorado, around 18,000 people show up every week! Munching on sweet corn-on-the-cob, we can begin to savor the value of creating strong, resilient local economies.

A fully realized close-to-home future will grow from these early shoots. Today even Boulder's thriving market provides less than 1 percent of the food consumed in the county; might that double in five years? In 10, grow tenfold? A group called Local Food Shift aims to do just that with its 10% Local Food Shift Pledge. Of course, except in our darkest futures, total local self-sufficiency is not the goal; each region will culti-vate and produce its own most abundant resources and products while continuing to engage with the global economy in a more balanced way than we do today. As the climate costs of long-distance transportation are factored into our markets, we may see revitalized regional and inter-regional commerce, offering exciting opportunities for growing all kinds of businesses.

In chapter 3 we sketched out some appealing, even essential, ways that people can invest using a close-to-home strategy. As more of us make a diligent commitment, here are some ways that we envision it showing up in our communities.

- An emphasis on personal resilience practices means that people will invest more of their time and attention in their homes and families. More people will look for ways to personally supply their basic needs such as energy and food, store rainwater or reuse graywater for irrigation, retrofit for energy efficiency, and add solar panels.

- Neighborhoods will take on renewed importance. People will invest more time getting to know their immediate environment and collaborating on projects that build social and tangible assets for all, such as open space and gardens. Systems such as "time

banks," as well as local currencies, will help foster the exchange
of skills and locally produced goods.

- Green building is likely to become the norm for commercial
  development and private homes, as the resultant energy savings
  increase over time; regional sourcing and reuse of materials may
  also support local economies.

- Building on today's fledgling efforts, new mechanisms will
  facilitate local investment, including community banks and
  loan funds, and perhaps the long-sought dream of local stock
  exchanges. Cities, counties, and states may join in these efforts
  by issuing publicly funded bonds for agricultural and green
  development purposes or by establishing publicly owned banks,
  as modeled by Bank of North Dakota.[1]

It is worth noting that some of the most innovative solutions to
issues such as climate change and poverty are taking root in cities, home
to more than half of the world's population. The title of a recent book, *If
Mayors Ruled the World*, encapsulates the idea that cities "are the primary
incubator of the cultural, social, and political innovations which shape
our planet." Author Benjamin Barber proposes a world Parliament of
Mayors, which would "enable cities to have a stronger voice in global
affairs, provide a worldwide platform for the sharing and transfer of urban
best practices, and establish a more democratic basis for addressing global
priorities than has ever existed."[2]

Much of the promise of the close-to-home strategy plays out at the
regional level. As local economies connect to create regional networks
and more capital stays closer to home, the possibilities for culturally
appropriate economic development and collaborative stewardship of local
natural resources are boundless. Expect to see energy systems decentralized through utility cooperatives and the production of biofuel, wind,
small-scale hydro, and solar power as well as proactive climate adapta-
tion (desalination in drought-hit coastal areas, forest and streamside

restoration in flood-prone areas). All of this builds resiliency as people exchange information, work together on projects, and, most of all, celebrate the land they call home.

Sustainable Global Economy Investing: Creating a Resilient Economy

Let's envision a future where people say, *Enough! We are not content to orient our lives or our society solely around the pursuit of wealth.* Other ecological and human values are equally important, and we want them all represented when we participate in the market. How might the global economy respond to an infusion of workers, consumers, and investors, all expressing their values through their financial decisions and expecting more—much more—from corporate interests?

One place we could look for change would be in the workplace itself. The pendulum is swinging back toward sharing both the responsibilities and the rewards of business. Surveys of the millennial generation show a marked desire to have their work reflect a sense of higher purpose. CEO salaries would come down from the extraordinary heights they have reached today. Discrimination of all stripes would diminish, while progressive companies that promote a healthy workplace will continue to attract the best talent.

We would also expect to see an expansion of how best to organize a business. Gar Alperovitz points out that there are already "more than 11,000 companies owned entirely or in significant part by some 13.6 million employees" and that cooperatives have "at least 130 million members (more than one in three Americans)."[3] The 1,000-and-counting certified B Corporations, including the authors' firm and the publisher of this book, will continue to grow at a rapid pace and will attract long-term investors who embrace their larger mission. "Conscious capitalism"[4] is another expression of the quest to embed a sense of higher purpose into corporate culture.

In the tangible realm, we would expect to see increased awareness about purchasing decisions. Information about any product or service is becoming ubiquitous, fed by peer-to-peer reviews and mobile technology. Companies will compete on a variety of factors, striving to demonstrate an authentic commitment to social and environmental values. This in turn bolsters the already-solid case for SRI, as companies that succeed at meeting genuine human needs become even more profitable while those that are seen as part of the problem are shunned.

With the workplace, marketplace, and investment arena all becoming values-oriented, the progression toward increased transparency and accountability will continue, including the evolution of more-uniform global standards. As SRI started gaining momentum in the 1990s and investors demanded that their investments take environmental, social, and governance issues into consideration, an entire industry emerged to monitor corporate behavior. Today companies find it much more difficult to hide behind a veil of secrecy, but compliance is still largely voluntary. It is likely that more of this kind of information will be required by regulatory agencies because this will be deemed as pertinent to disclose as financials are today.

Similarly, there will be increased pressure on government to step up to the policy plate, moving us forward on a wide range of issues. Wealth inequality, already a hot-button topic, will not abate until steps are taken that go beyond what is considered politically feasible today. Climate change is sure to reach a tipping point; even today many companies are clamoring for the United States to "put a price on carbon" so that businesses can know what the ground rules are. Once in place, today's wave of investments into renewable energy and efficiency solutions will grow exponentially, leading directly to an enduring increase of "green jobs" that helps to rejuvenate the middle class.

This society-wide embrace of a shared responsibility for the planet—and one another—could lead to solutions for today's seemingly intransigent problems. Tax reform could address inequality, penalize polluters, and reward productive innovation. The GDP, already seen by many as an insufficient indicator for measuring general well-being, would be dethroned by more-complete measures of how we are doing as a society.[5] All of this would, in turn, support even more private and public innovations that move us strongly in an upward direction, one that blends right into the transformative and the evolutionary.

Evolutionary Investing: Creating a Resilient World

What then might a surge of evolutionary investing bring to the future? This could be a very short section because the only possible answer is *Who knows?* Complexity theorist Stuart Kauffman, in *Reinventing the Sacred,* puts it this way: "This web of life, the most complex system we know of in the universe, breaks no law of physics, yet is partially lawless, ceaselessly creative.... This creativity is stunning, awesome, and worthy of reverence."[6]

This is the story of life itself, a strategy with a 3.8 billion–year track record. Putting attention and capital into evolutionary investing is a conscious decision to participate in this ageless process, helping spur the evolution of our society into something new. Here we follow the promising threads of profound and gentler technologies, re-envision governments and economies to be more responsive and respectful, and challenge ourselves to see what is over the horizon, boldly following the true north of our inner compass.

If significant numbers of people embrace this strategy as a piece of their overall resilient investing plan, the pace of innovation and the discovery of new solutions would surely accelerate. The generative potential of human society will foster new forms and structures that better meet the social and ecological imperatives of our time.

Although the outcomes of emergence cannot be predicted, inquiring minds yearn to glimpse at least the contours of what might appear. Science-fiction writers and futurists immerse themselves in these ideas, offering portraits of worlds and societies that most of us find difficult to imagine. We have already discussed the fact that virtually every field of human activity is ripe for reinvention, as our technologies, social contracts, and individual consciousness continue to unfold.

Rather than speculate on specifics, let's focus on what an evolutionary perspective suggests about the overall direction of change. To do this we call on several compelling models that map out a progression of developmental stages seen in both individuals and societies. Psychologist Clare Graves's research in this area has been popularized through Don Beck's spiral dynamics model and Ken Wilber's integral theory. In its simplest expression, human and social development suggests an inner evolution: An infant is completely self-absorbed, or egocentric. As we grow we identify with our family or tribe and become ethnocentric. Today a growing number of people have moved to the next stage and identify primarily as worldcentric.

A recent application of this theory applies it to economies. In *MEMEnomics: The Next-Generation Economic System,* Said Dawlabani asserts that our current economic system is in a process of decay, being replaced by a new, emerging system designed around natural principles that is better at distributing wealth and the benefits of innovation. It is both local and global at the same time, relying on a vast infrastructure of informed global citizens.[7]

Central to societal evolution is the increasing penetration of technology into all realms of our existence. The ability to publish, share, and spread new ideas has never been easier; in the realms of politics and the economy, the power of networked individuals will continue to grow. Likewise, this global perceptual system is seeping through many of the walls of corporate and government secrecy. While we have seen that these capacities can be abused, the democratization of information holds the promise of fueling the emergence of more-egalitarian values, such as we've seen in recent years with the focus on wealth inequality and the unmasking of the security state.

Jeremy Rifkin starts his latest book by saying, "The capitalist era is passing...not quickly, but inevitably. A new economic paradigm—the Collaborative Commons—is rising in its wake that will transform our way of life."[8] Indeed we can see the old model of competing self-interests, one fostered by "invisible hand" precepts, shifting toward an invisible heart approach of lateral networks that reward one's contribution to the common good. More people are coming to realize how entwined we are "with one another and with the geochemistry of the planet in a rich and complex choreography that sustains life itself."[9] This growing empathic awareness exerts an irrepressible tug, calling on each of us to play our part in ensuring the well-being of future generations and the biosphere.

～

With all three strategies rooted in ecological principles, we will see a regeneration of our planet's life-support systems. It is within our reach to alleviate poverty, hunger, and drinking-water shortages and to guarantee healthcare to all of humanity as a basic right. As more people take on a worldcentric identity, it is quite possible that we will shift some power away from the nation-state and toward both local and global entities that are better scaled to manage the tasks at hand. If it all comes together, we will find our way through the ultimate quandary of our times, building a thriving society that leaves vibrant habitats, healthy rivers and oceans, and a stable climate as our legacy to our children.

These musings are of course only a sliver of what is possible in a future where each of the three resilient investment strategies becomes widely adopted. We have barely touched on the synergies between any two, much less all three of them. Indeed it is the powerful combination of all of them that will allow civilization to thrive—a world of strong regional economies, interacting with a more just and sustainable market economy, all moving toward a new system that emphasizes participation and collaboration. This is our vision of a resilient future, one that each of us can help create through our investment decisions.

In the end we are right where we started. The future is uncertain, and any pretense of knowing what's to come will be eviscerated by events we cannot imagine. And yet, we are all here, one day following another, called upon to make decisions and respond to changing times as best we can. We know that the challenges facing humanity are formidable. But if we were to sum up the promise of resilient investing, beyond its narrow purpose of serving investors, it is a framework that helps each of us contribute our unique gifts to the world. And that is a comforting thought to end with, knowing that we are all in this together, doing our part, and staying connected.

The Case for SRI

A S CHAMPIONS OF SUSTAINABLE AND RESPONSIBLE INVESTING FOR 25 years, we embrace the goal of bringing your financial investment portfolio into harmony with the choices you are making across the entire Resilient Investing Map. As we noted in chapter 3, we feel that in this time of global challenges, it is crucial for corporations, financial institutions, and investors to take responsibility for the social and environmental consequences of their actions. SRI's combination of community investing, positive and negative screening (filtering companies based on issues and activities investors wish to support or avoid), and shareholder advocacy (direct engagement with corporate management) has helped reform capitalism while providing investors with an avenue to bring their money and their values into closer alignment.

SRI emerged in the early 1970s as a protest against the Vietnam War and a desire to avoid investing in military contractors; today a wide array of environmental, social, and governance (ESG) factors are assessed by SRI and conventional money managers as metrics that add value to their investment selection process. Environmental and resource-related concerns are increasingly being seen by the financial world as risks to corporate strategy.

For example, companies may face price increases on crucial but scarce raw materials. In the case of fossil fuels, the value of proven reserves on their balance sheets may fall in value if there is a risk of their becoming "stranded assets" due to climate change realities. Investment analysts look for evidence that companies are paying heed to the warnings and adjusting their plans accordingly. In the social arena, safety, human rights, labor standards, workplace and board diversity, and all forms of employee and community relations criteria highlight quality management policies and practices that are material to the financial bottom line. Bloomberg LP, for example, whose data service is the mainstay for most US investment analysts, now features a complete database of ESG disclosures for 3,600 companies worldwide, and it is used by many of the giant brokerage houses as part of their investment decision-making toolkit.

The Growth of SRI

Likewise investor commitment has been growing steadily since SRI's humble beginnings. In 1985 there was about $200 billion invested using an SRI approach. In 2014, $6.57 trillion was involved in ESG integration and shareholder advocacy,[1] which represents 17 percent of all professionally managed assets in the market. In 1990 there were about a dozen SRI mutual funds; today there are more than 150 SRI mutual funds as well as ever more institutional money managers integrating ESG considerations, including nearly 200 pension funds, foundations, and universities.

Venture capital and private investing using social and environmental filters is also mushrooming, according to the US SIF Foundation. There is now more than $130 billion in 300 private equity and venture capital, responsible property, and hedge funds—a 250 percent growth rate since 2010. Meanwhile about $60 billion is invested in more than 1,000 community development financial institutions that help revitalize underserved low-income communities.[2]

In the 1980s SRI began offering options for investing in local communities. Today this can be done almost everywhere in the United

States and in many places around the world. Social entrepreneurs are pumping capital into "the bottom of the pyramid" (the economies in megaslums and rural villages worldwide), shareholders are challenging corporate boards with resolutions calling for sustainable practices, and many Americans responded to the call to "move your money" by pulling out of big banks and piling into local financial institutions and online microfinance platforms.

Heart Rating

Of course, SRI mutual funds vary greatly in their approaches to responsibility. To help investors identify mutual funds that share their priorities, since 1992 we have maintained and published the Natural Investments Social Rating of about 120 domestic SRI funds. This rating, found on our website as well as at SustainabilityInvestor.com, ranks funds on a scale of one to five hearts based on the breadth and the depth of screening criteria, shareholder advocacy involvement, and commitment to supporting communities with their cash position.

Performance

Though initially ignored by much of Wall Street and attacked by others, by most objective measures SRI has been far more successful than was predicted by the naysayers. From 1992 to 1999, our own Jack Brill participated in a seven-year investment study by the *New York Times*. The only SRI advisor in the study, Jack earned a 17 percent annual return over the period using his models, only 0.5 percent off the top performer and well ahead of the bottom two participants. This served as a very public demonstration of how one could narrow his investment selection using social criteria without inherently compromising his financial return.

This has been affirmed by the performance of the Domini 400 Social Index, the first SRI index to be modeled after the S&P 500, which has outperformed the S&P for the nearly 25 years since it was launched (it is now called the MSCI KLD 400 Social Index).

Globally, in 2012 Deutsche Bank Group Climate Change Advisors analyzed more than 100 studies and found that incorporating ESG data in investment analysis is "correlated with superior risk-adjusted returns at a securities level."[3] These findings mirror a 2007 United Nations metastudy of 30 academic and industry studies.[4]

Policy

In recent years the growth of SRI and the increasing embrace of social and environmental responsibility by major corporate powers have set the stage for the SRI industry to play an increasingly vocal role in Washington, DC, and in state capitals. US SIF: The Forum for Sustainable and Responsible Investment (the industry trade association), along with institutional and corporate players, regularly push both Congress and the Securities and Exchange Commission to enact rules and regulations that address key social and environmental concerns. This proactive, positive voice on such key issues as full implementation of Dodd-Frank reforms, funding for Environmental Protection Agency enforcement, and aggressive carbon reduction policies is yet another reason why we see SRI investing as a key part of a resilient investing portfolio.

The Investor's Eye

T HERE'S A PHRASE WE OFTEN USE: *APPLYING THE INVESTOR'S EYE.*
We use "the eye" to think about, analyze, and put in perspective our
financial choices as well as the personal and tangible investments we have
outlined in this book. This is of course a very quick introduction to a topic
that we have all given a lot of thought to over the years, but we wanted
to give you a flavor of the questions that we, as investment advisors, run
through when we are looking at new opportunities.

Certainly when buying a home or spending money for a college
education or thinking about any big purchase, we all know what it means
to think critically about these spending/investing decisions. Now we want
to turn this type of thinking toward decisions about our personal, social,
and community assets and the tangible things we buy with our money.
In general, applying the investor's eye means being more comprehensive
in your thinking: think about the money with some degree of financial
sophistication, think about how your decisions affect your family and
community, and think about how you are helping or hindering the
building of a better world. These elements of your big-picture perspective
can be addressed through three aspects of applying the investor's eye.

144

The First Scan: Do the Math

Doing the math means asking a series of questions: How much does it cost, either in time or cash? How—and when—does it pay off, as a monetary return, a tangible asset such as food or habitat (for you or for other species), or a personal return like community building, health, or peace of mind? We are regularly scanning for activities that require a small investment but provide a big return or "bang for the buck."

Our math also includes considering the community and ecological values expressed in an investment—it is a first-pass screen ensuring that everything we're doing is consistent with our core values of caring for people and planet. Suffice it to say that for us, negative social or environmental costs shift the balance as we consider the viability of investments.

The Second Scan: Risk

While the Resilient Investing Map was designed as a response to systemic risk, it is important to remember that everything entails risk, even doing nothing, so the question is, *What risks and how risky?*

Recognize that each zone in our matrix, and any specific activity you engage in within a zone, carries its own inherent risks and rewards. Besides the usual litany of financial risks,[1] you will want to consider some fresh perspectives on risk as well. Tangible assets can degrade with age, are susceptible to catastrophes like fire and severe weather, and might need to be left behind if you move. Changes in your health and deaths of key loved ones will surely affect your personal assets.

There is no way to avoid risk entirely; you can mitigate but not eliminate. So look at each of your new actions and ask, Could the investment go bad or be a waste of time, and, if so, how bad would that be? Are there any obvious problems to be on the lookout for, and how can you build in some adaptability if the problems arise? One final but crucial question we ask is, Does the investment pass the "sleep test"? Does it leave you feeling more at peace or keep you awake at night? No one needs more stress!

The Third Scan: Balance

The final component is to look for balance among the selected investment options. Obviously, the RIM offers far more choices than used in
traditional financial diversification. With our investor's eye, we also look
for correlations to other investments, which is a fancy way of saying that
we try to reduce some risks by including other investments that provide
a balance. Asset allocation is more art than science, balancing the spreadsheet factors with a sense of overall fitness.

The careful use of the RIM offers a way to balance your known risks
as well as currently unrecognized risks that could emerge in the future.
It is precisely this broadly applied diligence that propels you to become
a Dancer, moving your time, attention, and money around the map in
dynamic response to risks and opportunities.

The Resilient Investor
Online Resources

THE COMPANION WEBSITE TO THIS BOOK, RESILIENTINVESTOR.COM, offers in-depth and up-to-date guidance that can help you build on the ideas we introduce in these pages and apply them successfully in your own life.

While the book serves as a concise introduction to the resilient investing framework, the website builds on this by exploring key themes in more detail and providing current information about potential investments and resources for the nine zones of the Resilient Investing Map.

The website offers several downloadable RIMs, including blank ones for you to use as you work your way through your own inventory and planning, as well as examples of completed maps from a variety of types of investors and from readers of the book.

A central feature of the website is comprehensive resource sections for each of the nine zones of the RIM. You'll find links to articles and websites that will help with your self-education on new topics, as well as information about companies, projects, and organizations that may be of interest to you as you round out your own resilient investing plan. This material is regularly updated to reflect the best of current thinking and opportunities in each zone.

The ResilientInvestor.com blog discusses topics related to resiliency and the ways that we and others are working with the ideas presented in the book. As you become more deeply engaged in your own resilient investing process, this will be a place to keep your thinking fresh and engage with others.

In addition, the site offers a range of supplementary material that delves more deeply into topics covered briefly in the book. In particular you'll find an overview of what we call *The Story of Our Times,* which fleshes out the social context and the issues of complexity, unpredictability, and uncertainty that informed our creation of the RIM.

Another essential supplement takes a closer look at each of the four scenarios (breakdown, muddle through down, muddle through up, and breakthrough). This section of the site features links to articles and videos from leading voices for each of these possible futures; these may be especially useful as you take that honest look at your own biases and beliefs that we asked of you. As a final step in this process, we offer a questionnaire that will help you determine which D-type best reflects your sense of how the future may unfold.

We look forward to hearing from you as we join together to blaze the early trails across this new landscape of resilient investing!

Notes

INTRODUCTION

Standing Up to Uncertainty

1. Robert Safian, "Generation Flux," *Huffington Post,* January 18, 2012, http://www.huffingtonpost.com/robert-safian/generation-flux_b_1213956.html (accessed August 28, 2014).

2. Tom Rosseen, "On Strong Equity Returns, Investors Are Slowly Reentering the Market," Lipper Mutual Fund Report Advertising supplement, Wall Street Journal online, March 15, 2013, http://online.wsj.com/ad/article/lipperawards-reentering (accessed August 28, 2014).

3. Doug Short, "The S&P 500, Dow and Nasdaq since Their 2000 Highs," Advisor Perspectives, July 6, 2014, http://www.advisorperspectives.com/dshort/commentaries/SPX-Dow-Nasdaq-Since-Their-2000-Highs.php (accessed August 28, 2014).

4. Andrew Zolli and Ann Marie Healy, *Resilience: Why Things Bounce Back* (New York: Free Press, 2012), Kindle Edition, 7.

5. Mark Drajem, "Obama Seeks to Boost Resilience to Climate-Driven Drought, Fires," Bloomberg News, March 4, 2014, http://www.bloomberg.com/news/2014-03-05/obama-seeks-to-boost-resilience-to-climate-driven-drought-fires.html (accessed August 26, 2014).

6. Try doing an online image search on the word *resilience* to get an eyeful of fascinating graphics!

7. William McDonough and Michael Braungart, *The Upcycle: Beyond Sustainability—Designing for Abundance* (New York: North Point Press, 2013), Kindle edition, 423.

8. Zolli and Healy, 21.

9. Rosabeth Moss Kanter, "Surprises Are the New Normal; Resilience Is the New Skill," *Harvard Business Review Blog Network*, July 17, 2013, http:// blogs.hbr.org/2013/07/surprises-are-the-new-normal-r (accessed August 26, 2014).

10. See http://www.naturalinvestments.com (accessed August 26, 2014).

CHAPTER 1

Facing the Future

1. This reference spurred some historical debate among our learned manuscript reviewers; while the phrase is often credited to Cervantes (as either the original source or repeated by him in *Don Quixote*), some claim it is an artifact of one translation and does not appear in the original. We are going with the good story here and letting the phrase be part of his canon.

2. Mark Twain, *The Tragedy of Pudd'nhead Wilson,* http://www.cs.cofc .edu/~manaris/books/Mark-Twain-The-Tragedy-of-Puddnhead-Wilson .txt (accessed August 26, 2014).

3. Classic diversification includes bond funds of various kinds (private, government); stock funds, including small-cap, mid-cap, and large-cap funds; global and domestic funds; index funds; and sector-specific funds; as well as a portion of your portfolio in "safe" savings vehicles such as CDs. Beyond these core holdings, a plethora of other financial vehicles are part of global markets, including real estate investment trusts, commodity investments, and many risk-trading products.

4. See http://www.investopedia.com/terms/s/systematicrisk.asp. There are "hedging" strategies designed to mitigate systemic risk, but they are not generally used by average investors (accessed August 26, 2014).

5. "How Gold Performs during a Financial Crash," *Seeking Alpha*, http://seeking alpha.com/article/295567-how-gold-performs-during-a-financial-crash (accessed August 26, 2014).

CHAPTER 2

More Than Money: Recognizing Your *Real* Net Worth

1. The origins of SRI, initially known as *socially responsible investing* and now known as *sustainable and responsible investing,* are fully explored in Hal Brill, Jack A. Brill, and Cliff Feigenbaum, *Investing with Your Values: Making Money and Making a Difference* (Bloomberg Press, 1999; New Society Press, 2000).

2. Learn about CSA farms and find one near you at http://www.localharvest
.org/csa (accessed August 26, 2014).

3. A good overview as of early 2013 is here: http://www.economist.com/news
/leaders/21573104-internet-everything-hire-rise-sharing-economy (accessed
August 26, 2014). Search the term *sharing economy* online for a wide range
of more recent articles and commentary.

4. Elizabeth Scott, "Benefits of Altruism," About.com, http://stress.about.com
/od/lowstresslifestyle/a/altruism.htm (accessed August 26, 2014).

5. See Sean Esbjorn-Hargens, "An Overview of Integral Theory," Integral Life,
March 12, 2009, http://integrallife.com/integral-post/overview-integral
-theory (accessed August 26, 2014).

CHAPTER 3

Weaning off Wall Street

1. Lucy Jay-Kennedy, "New Report: Bringing Impact Investing from the
Margins to the Mainstream," World Economic Forum, September 19, 2013,
http://www.weforum.org/news/new-report-bringing-impact-investing
-margins-mainstream (accessed August 26, 2014).

2. Katie Escherich and Bianna Golodryga, "Warren Buffett's Investment Advice
for You," ABC News, July 10, 2009, http://abcnews.go.com/GMA/Business
/story?id=8041663&page=1 (accessed August 28, 2014).

3. Don Shaffer, "What's Next? Local Investing," GreenMoney Journal, http://
archives.greenmoneyjournal.com/article.mpl?newsletterid=51&article
id=736 (accessed August 28, 2014).

4. Ibid.

5. Michael Shuman, *Local Dollars, Local Sense: How to Shift Your Money from
Wall Street to Main Street and Achieve Real Prosperity* (Community Resilience Guides) (White River Junction: Chelsea Green, 2012), xx.

6. See especially *Guide to Going Local*, produced by the Center for a New
American Dream (http://www.newdream.org/programs/collaborative
-communities/community-action-kit/local), and the work of Business Alliance for Local Living Economies (https://bealocalist.org) (both accessed
August 26, 2014).

7. Among those preparing for breakdown within a larger, collaborative framework are the UK-based Dark Mountain Project (http://dark-mountain
.net) and John Robb's Resilient Communities (http://www.resilient
communities.com). The Transition Town network (http://transitionus.org

/transition-town-movement) focuses on preparing for energy disruptions though generally not so much for a full breakdown (all accessed August 26, 2014).

8. James Wesley Rawles, *How to Survive the End of the World as We Know It: Tactics, Techniques, and Technologies for Uncertain Times* (New York: Plume, 2009).

9. Center for a New American Dream, *Guide to Going Local*, 1.

10. John Robb, "The Big Reset. Don't Get Left Behind," Resilient Communities, June 2, 2012, resilientcommunities.com/the-big-reset (accessed August 26, 2014).

11. James Wesley Rawles outlines his "Rawlesian Survival Mind-Set," which includes charity by emphasizing that one's personal preparation must include a readiness to be of service to others who may be less prepared for the scale of changes taking place.

12. David Holmgren and Ian Lillington, *Energy Descent Action Planning for Hepburn Shire,* October 2011, http://www.hepburn.vic.gov.au/files/20-03 -2012Attachment10-EnergyDescentActionPlanning-HolmgrenDesign ServiceFinalReport.pdf (accessed August 26, 2014).

13. Hazel Henderson, "What's Wrong with Market Economics and GDP?" Inter-Press Service, April 30, 2008, www.hazelhenderson.com/2008/04/30/whats -wrong-with-market-economics-and-gdp-april-2008/ (accessed August 26, 2014).

14. See http://www.youtube.com/watch?v=DOZzNOkcEgM for some good memories (accessed August 26, 2014).

15. For example, consumers can easily see which clothing manufacturers have signed on to the strictest operational guidelines in Bangladesh by visiting http://www.cleanclothes.org/issues/faq-safety-accord (accessed August 26, 2014).

16. See http://gofossilfree.org (accessed August 26, 2014).

17. See http://www.greenamerica.org/fossilfree (accessed August 26, 2014).

18. See http://breakupwithyourmegabank.org (accessed August 26, 2014).

19. Ana Bernasek, "The Typical Household, Now Worth a Third Less," New York Times online, July 26, 2014, http://www.nytimes.com/2014/07/27 /business/the-typical-household-now-worth-a-third-less.html?_r=0 (accessed August 26, 2014).

20. Carter Phipps, *Evolutionaries: Unlocking the Spiritual and Cultural Potential of Science's Greatest Idea* (New York: Harper Perennial, 2012), 18.

21. Ibid, 44.

22. Ibid, 44.

23. David Korten, "A New Story for a New Economy," YES! Magazine online, March 19, 2014, http://www.yesmagazine.org/happiness/a-new-story-for-a-new-economy (accessed August 26, 2014).

24. Charles Eisenstein, *Sacred Economics: Money, Gift, and Society in the Age of Transition* (Berkeley: Evolver Editions, 2011), 437.

25. Elon Reeve Musk is CEO and chief product architect of Tesla Motors as well as chairman of SolarCity; see http://en.wikipedia.org/wiki/Elon_Musk (accessed August 26, 2014).

26. Hunter Lovins and John Fullerton, "Transforming Finance and the Regenerative Economy," GreenMoney Journal, January 2014, http://www.green moneyjournal.com/january-2014/transforming-finance (accessed August 26, 2014).

27. Good places to start include http://www.singularityhub.com, http://www .longnow.org, and http://www.wired.com (all accessed August 26, 2014).

28. See http://www.ted.com/speakers/amory_lovins (accessed August 26, 2014).

29. See http://www.ted.com/talks/peter_diamandis_abundance_is_our_future (accessed August 26, 2014).

30. Buckminster Fuller Institute, http://bfi.org/dymaxion-forum/2012/05 /making-world-work (accessed September 26, 2014).

31. See Hal Brill, Jack A. Brill, and Cliff Feigenbaum, *Investing with Your Values: Making Money and Making a Difference* (Bloomberg Press, 1999), 93: "In fact, Smith was a moral philosopher; his writings speak of ethics, not mechanical functionings of the market. Smith envisioned a world populated by persons steeped with strong morals, who understood that enlightened self-interest includes notions of social equity.…His faith in the invisible hand was predicated on economies operating at personal scales, unhampered by government or corporate manipulation. In his time, when economies operated primarily on a local scale, such a view was idealist, yet within reach."

32. Bruce Bartlett, "'Financialization' as a Cause of Economic Malaise," New York Times online, June 6, 2011, http://economix.blogs.nytimes.com/2013/06/11 /financialization-as-a-cause-of-economic-malaise (accessed August 26, 2014).

CHAPTER 4

A Field Guide to Resilient Investing

1. Ralph Waldo Emerson, *The Conduct of Life*, "II: Power," 1860, http://www
.emersoncentral.com/power.htm (accessed August 30, 2014).

2. There are countless resources to inform this process, including the
classic *What Color Is Your Parachute?* (updated annually; see http://www
.jobhuntersbible.com and http://www.amazon.com/What-Color-Your
-Parachute-2014/dp/1607743620) and Integral Life Practice (see http://www
.integral-life-practice.com) (all accessed August 26, 2014).

3. See http://www.bcorporation.net (accessed August 26, 2014).

4. Laurie Bassi, "The Impact of U.S. Firms' Investments in Human Capital on
Stock Prices," Bassi Investments, June 2004, http://www.mtdiabloastd.org
/Resources/Documents/Meetings/2010-07%20Gina%20Jesse%20Impact
%20on%20Stock%202004%20research-Bassi.pdf (accessed August 26, 2014).

5. US SIF, The Forum for Sustainable and Responsible Investment, compiles
biannual reports. For a list of recent reports, see http://www.ussif.org
/content.asp?contentid=82; for more about shareholder resolutions, see
http://www.ussif.org/content.asp?contentid=67 (both accessed August 26,
2014).

6. See http://www.ted.com/talks/william_mcdonough_on_cradle_to_cradle
_design.html (accessed August 26, 2014).

7. Michael Litchfield, *In-Laws, Outlaws, and Granny Flats: Your Guide to
Turning One House into Two Homes* (Newtown, CT: Taunton Press, 2011).

8. A key popularizer of tiny houses is http://www.tumbleweedhouses.com
(accessed August 26, 2014).

9. Paul Hawken, Amory Lovins, and L. Hunter Lovins, *Natural Capitalism*
(Snowmass, CO: Rocky Mountain Institute), http://www.natcap.org/images
/other/NCchapter6.pdf (accessed August 26, 2014).

10. See http://www.builditsolar.com, an excellent free resource on how to
approach comprehensive energy efficiency. See the "Half Program" on how
they reduced energy use by 50 percent (accessed August 26, 2014).

11. See http://www.localharvest.org/csa to search for a CSA in your area
(accessed August 26, 2014).

12. Here is one recent overview: http://www.economist.com/news/leaders
/21573104-internet-everything-hire-rise-sharing-economy (accessed
August 26, 2014).

13. Duane Elgin's 1981 book *Voluntary Simplicity,* revised in 2010, offers a good introduction: http://duaneelgin.com/books/voluntary-simplicity (accessed August 26, 2014).

14. See http://simplicitycollective.com/start-here/what-is-voluntary-simpli city-2 and http://www.choosingvoluntarysimplicity.com (both accessed August 26, 2014).

15. See http://www.politifact.com/texas/statements/2013/nov/25/senfronia -thompson/macys-other-retailers-asked-rick-perry-veto-equal-/ (accessed August 26, 2014).

16. See http://www.greenamerica.org/programs/responsibleshopper and http:// www.goodguide.com/about/mobile (both accessed August 26, 2014).

17. The Center for a New American Dream has put together an online Conscious Consumer Shopping Guide that highlights key environmental concerns and many resources for more information on nearly two dozen types of products, from baby food to batteries: http://www.newdream.org/programs /beyond-consumerism/rethinking-stuff/buy-green. Several green consumer organizations offer member directories: Green America's http://greenpages .org; LOHAS at http://www.lohas.com/lohas-business-directory; coopera- tive businesses of all types at the National Cooperative Business Associa- tion's CooperateUSA mobile app (http://531251-dbl.mindactive.com/down load_app); B Corps at http://bcorporation.net; and the Green Restaurant Association at http://www.dinegreen.com (all accessed August 26, 2014).

18. Search online for details about various types of product certifications, including certified organic, fair trade, cruelty-free, GMO-free, ISO 14000, Green Seal, ULE 880, greenhouse gas corporate standards, Global Reporting Initiative, and Carbon Disclosure Project.

19. See http://www.fairgold.org, http://www.fairtrade.net/gold.html, and http:// www.communitymining.org/en/fairmined-gold (all accessed August 26, 2014).

20. Bill Mollison, *Permaculture: A Designer's Manual* (Tyalgum, NSW, Australia: Tagari, 1988).

21. See http://www.bioneers.org (accessed August 26, 2014).

22. Wendell Berry and Norman Wirzba, *The Art of the Commonplace: The Agrarian Essays of Wendell Berry* (Berkeley: Counterpoint Press, 2003), 46.

23. Woody Tasch, *Inquiries into the Nature of Slow Money: Investing as if Food, Farms, and Fertility Mattered* (White River Junction, VT: Chelsea Green, 2008).

24. Christopher and Barbara Johnson, "Menominee Forest Keepers," American Forests, Spring 2012, http://www.americanforests.org/magazine/article/menominee-forest-keepers (accessed August 26, 2014).

25. See http://www.growingpower.org (accessed August 26, 2014).

26. The Quivira Coalition has long been a leader in these efforts; see http://www.quiviracoalition.org (accessed August 26, 2014).

27. See https://slowmoney.org/local-groups (accessed August 26, 2014).

28. See https://credibles.org (accessed August 26, 2014).

29. See http://biomimicry.net/about/biomimicry/case-examples (accessed August 26, 2014).

30. See 20 surprisingly complex objects made with 3D printing at http://www.hongkiat.com/blog/3d-printings (accessed August 26, 2014).

31. Michael Bauwens, "Jeremy Rifkin's Distributed Capitalism Scenario," P2P Foundation, May 14, 2013, http://blog.p2pfoundation.net/jeremy-rifkins-distributed-capitalism-scenario/2013/05/14 (accessed September 1, 2014).

32. For a good intro, see Noelle Swan, "The 'Maker Movement' Creates D.I.Y. Revolution," Christian Science Monitor online, July 6, 2014, http://www.csmonitor.com/Innovation/2014/0706/The-maker-movement-creates-D.I.Y.-revolution (accessed September 1, 2014).

33. Bloomberg now offers an ESG data service, including multiyear data reported by more than 3,600 companies worldwide; this service is used by many of the major brokerage houses as part of their investment decision-making toolkit.

34. Antony Bugg-Levine and Jed Emerson, *Impact Investing: Transforming How We Make Money while Making a Difference* (San Francisco: Jossey-Bass, 2011), 8.

35. For more on these developments, see James Frazier, "Goldman, Morgan Stanley Launch Social Impact Funds," Natural Investments, December 4, 2013, http://naturalinvesting.com/blog/2013/12/goldman-morgan-stanley-launch-social-impact-funds/ (accessed September 1, 2014).

36. Impact Hub (http://www.impacthub.net), which supports 50 hubs on six continents and 30 more in the development phase, is but one example (accessed August 26, 2014).

37. See https://joinmosaic.com, http://sunfunder.com, http://greenzu.com/crowdfunded-solar, http://solarcity.com, and https://www.abundancegeneration.com (all accessed August 26, 2014).

38. Good places to start include http://www.impactinvestingdirectory.com
and Global Impact Investing Rating Systems (http://www.giirs.org) (both
accessed August 26, 2014).

CHAPTER 6

Be Ready for Anything

1. "The Tao Te Ching by Lao Tzu, The Witter Bynner Version," Terebess
Asia Online, http://terebess.hu/english/tao/bynner.html#Kap22 (accessed
September 2, 2014).

2. James Howard Kunstler, *The Long Emergency: Surviving the End of Oil,
Climate Change, and Other Converging Catastrophes of the Twenty-First
Century* (New York: Grove Press, 2005).

3. See Paul Kingsnorth of the UK Dark Mountain project (http://dark
-mountain.net and http://www.orionmagazine.org/index.php/mag/con
tributor/7312) and the Transition Network (http://www.transitionnetwork
.org and http://www.transitionus.org/transition-towns). Derrick Jensen is
a related though harder-edged voice: http://www.orionmagazine.org/index
.php/mag/contributor/4698 (all accessed September 2, 2014).

4. John Mauldin, "The Muddle Through Economy," Mauldin Economics,
May 30, 2003, http://www.mauldineconomics.com/frontlinethoughts
/the-muddle-through-economy-mwo053003 (accessed September 2, 2014).

5. E-mail conversation with the authors, February 11, 2013.

6. Jamais Cascio, "Bots, Bacteria and Carbon," Ensia.com, March 29, 2013,
http://ensia.com/videos/bots-bacteria-and-carbon (accessed September 2,
2014).

7. Professional futurists and scenario planners take the process we introduce
here into much more detail. See, for example, the scenario planning under-
taken by Peter Schwartz, Jamais Cascio, or David Holmgren. In particular,
they all look much more closely at variations within our simpler muddle
through up/down scenarios, exploring the implications of specific kinds
of environmental pressures and social responses. See also Adam Kahane,
Transformative Scenario Planning: Working Together to Change the Future
(San Francisco: Berrett-Koehler, 2012).

8. Jamais Cascio, "Bots, Bacteria and Carbon," Ensia.com, March 29, 2013,
http://ensia.com/videos/bots-bacteria-and-carbon (accessed September 2,
2014).

9. "Politics of Science Fiction: Kim Stanley Robinson," TTBOOK, April 13, 2014, http://www.ttbook.org/book/politics-science-fiction-kim-stanley -robinson (accessed August 26, 2014).

10. See http://transitionvoice.com/2011/11/three-paths-to-near-term-human -extinction and http://guymcpherson.com/guest-commentaries (accessed August 26, 2014).

11. Check out Ray Kurzweil's worldview in "Immortality by 2015," June 21, 2013, http://www.kurzweilai.net/global-futures-2045-ray-kurzweil-immortality -by-2045 (accessed August 26, 2014).

12. See http://en.wikiquote.org/wiki/William_Gibson (accessed August 26, 2014).

CHAPTER 8

Your Resilient Investing Plan

1. Howard Rheingold offers a detailed guide to doing just this: "Crap Detection 101," June 30, 2009, http://blog.sfgate.com/rheingold/2009/06/30/crap -detection-101 (accessed August 26, 2014).

CHAPTER 9

Tales of Resilient Living

1. See http://www.ted.com/speakers/hans_rosling (accessed September 3, 2014).

CHAPTER 10

The Invisible Heart of Resilience

1. For more on this movement, see http://publicbankinginstitute.org (accessed August 26, 2014).

2. Benjamin R. Barber, *If Mayors Ruled the World: Dysfunctional Nations, Rising Cities* (New Haven, CT: Yale University Press, 2013), http://benjaminbarber .org/books/if-mayors-ruled-the-world (accessed October 7, 2014).

3. Gar Alperovitz, "The New-Economy Movement," GarAlperovitz.com, July 7, 2011, http://www.garalperovitz.com/2011/07/the-new-economy-movement -the-nation-2011 (accessed August 26, 2014).

4. See http://www.consciouscapitalism.org (accessed August 26, 2014).

5. See the Calvert-Henderson Quality of Life Indictors at http://www.calvert
   -henderson.com (accessed August 26, 2014).

6. Stuart A. Kauffman, *Reinventing the Sacred: A New View of Science, Reason,
   and Religion* (New York: Basic Books, 2010), xi.

7. Jeff Salzman, "A Review of MEMEnomics: The Next Generation Economic
   System," Daily Evolver, January 14, 2014, http://www.dailyevolver
   .com/2014/01/review-of-memenomics-the-next-generation-economic
   -system (accessed August 26, 2014).

8. Jeremy Rifkin, *The Zero Marginal Cost Society: The Internet of Things, the
   Collaborative Commons, and the Eclipse of Capitalism* (New York: Palgrave
   Macmillan, 2014), 1.

9. Jeremy Rifkin, *The Empathic Civilization: The Race to Global Consciousness
   in a World in Crisis* (New York: Tarcher, 2009), 598.

RESOURCE 1
The Case for SRI

1. US SIF Foundation, "Report on Sustainable and Responsible Investing
   Trends in the United States," 2014, http://www.ussif.org/trends (accessed
   November 21, 2014).

2. Ibid.

3. DB Climate Change Advisors, "Sustainable Investing: Establishing Long-
   Term Value and Performance," June 2012, https://www.dbadvisors.com
   /content/_media/Sustainable_Investing_2012.pdf (accessed August 26, 2014).

4. UNEP Finance Initiative and Mercer, "Demystifying Responsible Invest-
   ment Performance: A Review of Key Academic and Broker Research on
   ESG Factors," October 2007, http://www.unepfi.org/fileadmin/documents
   /Demystifying_Responsible_Investment_Performance_01.pdf (accessed
   August 26, 2014).

RESOURCE 2
The Investor's Eye

1. A good overview is here: "Risk and Diversification: Different Types of
   Risk," Investopedia, http://www.investopedia.com/university/risk/risk2.asp
   (accessed August 26, 2014).

Glossary

accredited investor   an individual or institution qualified to invest in certain unregistered private securities; the law requires that such an investor have a liquid net worth (excluding primary residence) of $1 million or an annual income of $200,000 per year in each of the past two tax years ($300,000 if married)

angel investor   an accredited investor who invests in private companies primarily in the startup phase of their development

Anthropocene   a term coined in the 1980s to describe the current geological period that commenced during the Industrial Revolution, in which mankind is the dominant influence on changes to the natural world; it is widely used in a sociological context and is being actively discussed by geologists

B Corp   one of more than 1,000 companies certified by the rating agency B Lab as meeting a minimum number of superior social, environmental, and governance policies and practices that are beneficial to owners, employees, communities, customers, and the environment

biomimicry   a process of using the patterns and principles of nature to design human technologies and systems

blessedness   in the book's context, a term used by Aristotle to describe the pursuit of a happy and virtuous life

bowing to the bottom line   the tendency to prioritize financial profit or investment return without consideration of material environmental, social, or governance factors

breakdown/long emergency   a global scenario that describes social, economic, and/or environmental meltdown, leaving the global economy in tatters

breakthrough/rational emergence a global scenario that posits exponential social innovation, dramatic rise of new technologies, and the evolution of wisdom and consciousness to deploy them wisely

circular economy an industrial economy based on the use of biological materials and regenerative processes that are biodegradable, that minimize harmful waste, and that cycle by-products into usable goods

close-to-home strategy the process of financial and nonfinancial investing in one's personal health and well-being, home and neighborhood, social relationships, and local community

Community Emergency Response Team (CERT) a program that educates people about disaster preparedness for hazards that may impact their area and trains them in basic disaster response skills, such as fire safety, light search and rescue, team organization, and disaster medical operations

community investing investments primarily in community development banks, credit unions, loan funds, venture capital, and microfinance institutions that provide low-income and other marginalized people with access to capital for housing, entrepreneurship, and community economic development purposes

community resilience the degree to which a community has prepared for economic and ecological challenges and transitioned to a more self-reliant and viable local economy; increased resilience is often achieved by way of a cooperative strategic-planning process involving a wide range of local stakeholders

community-supported agriculture (CSA) a local share-based farming model where customers purchase a monthly or annual share of whatever is produced by the farm and receive produce on a weekly basis

confirmation bias the tendency to interpret new information as confirmation of existing beliefs or theories

conservation finance the use of debt and equity capital, tax incentives, and market mechanisms to secure, manage, and conserve land and water ecosystems

crowdfunding a method employed by startup companies and projects to raise capital from individual investors in small amounts, usually through online platforms

distributed manufacturing the process of producing goods in a decentralized manner rather than in large industrial manufacturing facilities (e.g., 3D printing)

diversification the process of allocating assets across a wide array of investment categories, primarily to mitigate risk

D-type the personality archetype system in *The Resilient Investor* that illustrates one's assessment of our future scenarios (e.g., Doomer, Dreamer, Dancer)

environmental ethics the use of ethical criteria that consider the rights of ecosystems and other species to protect and preserve their existence and integrity

environmental, social, and governance (ESG) practices the practices used by companies to demonstrate responsibility to employees, customers, communities, and the environment, such as ensuring safe and healthy working conditions, providing adequate wages and benefits, ensuring diversity in the workplace and on boards of directors, and addressing climate change and other forms of environmental risk; some investment managers select portfolio companies based on these criteria

evolutionary spirituality secular spiritual practice using an array of ancient Eastern and innovative Western techniques, rituals, and traditions, as well as the insights of modern science, for personal and cultural transformation

evolutionary strategy investment approaches across all asset categories that use innovative techniques and methods to transform our spiritual and psychological lives, regenerate natural systems, and redesign social and economic systems

exchange-traded funds (ETFs) a pooled investment of stocks, bonds, or commodities similar to a mutual fund but which trades on an exchange like an individual stock

externalities the costs or benefits of economic activity that affect society or the environment but are not accounted for in the price of goods and services or in the internal accounting of companies producing goods and services (e.g., pollution)

financial assets cash or other monetary instruments that can be purchased and saved or traded as investments

fossil fuel–free an investment screening method that removes fossil fuel exploration, production, and distribution companies from an investment portfolio

future-proofing the process of implementing an array of strategies to prepare for and adapt to a variety of possible scenarios in the hopes of being able to thrive under any circumstances

green jobs career opportunities in sustainability-oriented fields, such as renewable energy, building construction, and industrial processes

Heart Rating the system developed and maintained by Natural Investments since 1992 that rates sustainable and responsible mutual funds on the breadth and depth of their environmental, social, and governance criteria as well as their participation in community investing and shareholder engagement; it is published at NaturalInvestments.com and Sustainability Investor.com; also known as *NI Social Rating*

impact investing a component of sustainable and responsible investing that channels private debt and equity to entrepreneurial startup companies, organizations, and projects that have a measurable beneficial impact on social and environmental challenges and solutions

integral theory a philosophy developed by Ken Wilber and others that intends to be a comprehensive, synthesizing, and transdisciplinary framework that incorporates science, emotional intelligence, and spiritual development; applicable to numerous fields of thought, including government, finance, and personal and professional growth

investing directing time, attention, energy, or money in ways that move us toward our future dreams, using a diverse range of strategies

investor's eye a metaphor for the analytical process used when evaluating potential investments

invisible heart a twist on Adam Smith's *invisible hand of the marketplace* adage suggesting that the social and environmental benefits of economic activity follow naturally from one's pursuit of individual resilience

lifestyle immunity the desire to live at the periphery of mainstream society through various forms of self-sufficiency in order to be less vulnerable to potential socioeconomic breakdown and to thrive in turbulent times

local investing debt and equity investments in local, typically small, businesses and community development projects

liquidity the quality of financial assets and investment instruments that allows them to be easily sold, typically in the capital markets, and converted to readily available cash

maker movement networks of do-it-yourself enthusiasts who use practical arts, tools, and technologies to invent, innovate, and inspire economic activity

microfinance   pools of investment capital typically lent by intermediaries in small amounts to low-income borrowers throughout the world for the purpose of starting or expanding businesses and revitalizing communities

muddle through down/relentless struggle   a global scenario that describes rolling recessions amid a failure to address the systemic causes of social, economic, and environmental decline

muddle through up/incremental progress   a global scenario that describes the gradual improvement of key quality of life indicators within the existing framework of political and economic systems

natural investing   an ethical method of investing coined by Natural Investments based on the principle that it is entirely natural to align one's values with one's investments

new normal   the description economists and others use to describe the uncertain, volatile swings and smaller long-term growth rate of the global economy since the economic downturn that began in 2007

permaculture   a system of designing all human activities based on the principles of natural systems, intended to establish a sustainable way of life based on "permanent agriculture"

personal assets   the skills, capacities, knowledge, and experience people possess to support personal and professional development, effective social relationships, and a strong, caring, and healthy community and society

"plan to plan" rule   an observation and a suggestion that one needs to schedule time with partners and associates to be able to schedule time for longer-term planning (e.g., "We need a meeting today to get ready for next week's meeting")

portfolio screening   the process used by investment managers to exclude and include companies based on environmental, social, and governance criteria, including specific economic sectors and company policies and practices

real net worth   an expanded notion of personal wealth that includes nonfinancial value such as strong social systems and personal, community, and environmental health

regenerative agriculture   a whole-systems approach to agriculture that eliminates the use of off-site energy and fertilizer, uses natural pest elimination strategies, and aligns with the fecundity of nature

regenerative investing   financial investments in natural resources that generate positive returns to people while providing long-term benefits to ecosystems (e.g., conservation finance, sustainable forestry and agriculture)

resilience   the capacity to thrive by anticipating and preparing for disturbance, improving the ability to withstand shocks, rebuilding as necessary, and adapting and evolving when possible

resilient investing   using time, attention, and energy to direct one's assets (personal, tangible, or financial), using a mix of close-to-home, sustainable global economy, and evolutionary strategies to further the investor's goals and to build a better world

Resilient Investing Map (RIM)   the framework developed in this book that describes the comprehensive approach to resilient investing, where the three investment strategies (close to home, sustainable global economy, and evolutionary) intersect with the three types of assets (personal, tangible, financial) to create nine zones of investment focus

scenario planning   a strategic-planning process that visualizes future conditions and events and presents unique stories of the future to enable decision makers to plan and adapt

sharing economy   economic, social, and technological systems that enable shared access to goods, services, information, and labor

show-me-the-money strategy   the pervasive, conventional investment strategy that places profit before all other values

Slow Money   an investment movement proposed and initiated by Woody Tasch in his 2008 book *Inquiries into the Nature of Slow Money* to steer investors toward placing capital with small farms and local food enterprises

social capital   the beneficial networks of relationships that exist among a group of people living in a community or society that help the community function effectively

social purpose bonds   a debt instrument that uses investor capital to support private organizations and companies in delivering social services for governments; also called social impact bonds

stop/start/sustain technique   a planning exercise that helps clarify and prioritize tasks, activities, or investments using three questions: *What are you going to stop doing? What are you going to start doing? What are you going to keep doing?*

stranded assets   assets that have suffered unanticipated or premature conversion to liabilities or a dramatic loss of value; in-ground fossil fuel resources are an example of potential stranded assets as actions to respond to global climate change increase

sustainability   as applied to humanity, the manner in which individual and collective choices consider people and the environment, allowing civilization to thrive in harmony with natural systems

sustainable and responsible investing (SRI)   the 45-year-old approach to integrating social and environmental values into the process of selecting investments that provide benefits to communities, employees, and nature as well as owners

sustainable global economy strategy   participation in the transnational corporate economy through employment, shopping, banking, and investing

systemic risk   the risk that is inherent to an entire market; also called *undiversifiable risk*

tangible assets   literally any property that can be physically touched, meaning real assets like a house, personal possessions, energy systems, gardens, and habitat/landscape

time bank   a system of local economic exchange that uses time as its measure of currency to purchase or exchange goods and services

transition town   a community resilience movement with chapters throughout the world that develops local strategic plans for how communities can adapt to climate change and the decline in the availability of fossil fuels and become more energy and food self-sufficient

triple bottom line   social, environmental, and economic business value, often described as "people, planet, and profit"

weaning off Wall Street   a phrase coined by the authors to describe the process of stepping away from traditional investment vehicles to seek diversification and return from alternatives

whole-systems thinking   a way of seeing everything as part of a system, solving problems and making decisions by looking at things in their entirety and in relationship to other elements, not as isolated parts

worldcentric   a term used to describe an advanced stage of ethical development, where a person is concerned with the welfare of all human beings

VUCA   acronym for *volatile, uncertain, complex,* and *ambiguous,* a description of the challenges of our times coined by the US military

Index

About
the Authors

THE AUTHORS OF *THE RESILIENT INVESTOR* ARE MANAGING PARTNERS of Natural Investments, LLC. Natural Investments is an investment advisory firm with nine offices in eight states and has been a leading voice in sustainable and socially responsible investing since the publication of co-founder Jack Brill's *Investing from the Heart* (Crown) in 1992.

Hal Brill is the co-author of *Investing with Your Values: Making Money and Making a Difference* (Bloomberg Press, 1999; New Society Press, 2000) and co-founder of Natural Investments. He lives in a sustainable neighborhood that he developed on the edge of Paonia, Colorado. He is on the board of Solar Energy International, which provides technical training in renewable energy, and is business manager of an organic hops farm.

Michael Kramer is director of social research at Natural Investments. He joined the firm in 2000 after being a client for 10 years. He serves on the Policy Committee of US SIF: The Forum for Sustainable and Responsible Investment. He publishes the Sustainable Shareholder column at GreenBiz.com and is a strong advocate of innovative financial instruments, local green economic development, and corporate and regulatory reform. He lives in Kailua-Kona, Hawaii.

Christopher Peck lives in Sonoma County, California, on a developing homestead within biking distance of a lovely downtown. He is a long-term sustainability entrepreneur and holistic financial planner. He has taught sustainable finance for many years, including in a green MBA program, and a popular course on business planning. He has a black belt in aikido and has been studying Zen Buddhism for more than 20 years.

Jim Cummings is a writer and editor who has worked with Natural Investments for the past 15 years. He is the founder of the Acoustic Ecology Institute, which offers clear, unbiased information on sound-related environmental issues, and he writes on the nature of our times at BrightBlueBall.net. He lives outside Santa Fe, New Mexico, along the Rio Galisteo in the southern foothills of the Rockies.

About
Natural Investments

NATURAL INVESTMENTS, LLC, IS AN INVESTMENT ADVISOR WITH financial professionals in nine offices across eight states. For more than 25 years, we have managed sustainable and responsible investing (SRI) portfolios for individuals, organizations, businesses, and institutions.

Natural Investments is an SRI thought leader, its principals having authored *Investing from the Heart: The Guide to Socially Responsible Investments and Money Management* (1992) and *Investing with Your Values: Making Money and Making a Difference* (1999). In addition to our portfolio management services, the firm is deeply committed to influencing corporate practices, channeling capital to low-income people and communities worldwide, and supporting the transition to a just, resilient, and locally vibrant economy. We regularly participate in shareholder advocacy and policy efforts aimed at protecting investors and stabilizing the financial system, and our advisors are active in their local communities.

The firm has maintained the NI Social Rating of domestic SRI mutual funds since 1992, offering investors an easy way to gauge the breadth and depth of funds' social and environmental criteria used to select portfolio companies (available at NaturalInvestments.com and SustainabilityInvestor.com).

A founding certified B Corp, the firm was recognized by B Lab in 2012 as "Best for the World" and in 2013 as "Best for Communities" for its triple-bottom-line policies and practices. Natural Investments donates 1 percent of its gross revenues to social and environmental causes and encourages its clients to devote a portion of their portfolio to community investing initiatives.

To learn more about our company and the services we offer, visit NaturalInvestments.com.

Berrett–Koehler
Publishers

Berrett-Koehler is an independent publisher dedicated to an ambitious mission: *Creating a World That Works for All*.

We believe that to truly create a better world, action is needed at all levels—individual, organizational, and societal. At the individual level, our publications help people align their lives with their values and with their aspirations for a better world. At the organizational level, our publications promote progressive leadership and management practices, socially responsible approaches to business, and humane and effective organizations. At the societal level, our publications advance social and economic justice, shared prosperity, sustainability, and new solutions to national and global issues.

A major theme of our publications is "Opening Up New Space." Berrett-Koehler titles challenge conventional thinking, introduce new ideas, and foster positive change. Their common quest is changing the underlying beliefs, mindsets, institutions, and structures that keep generating the same cycles of problems, no matter who our leaders are or what improvement programs we adopt.

We strive to practice what we preach—to operate our publishing company in line with the ideas in our books. At the core of our approach is stewardship, which we define as a deep sense of responsibility to administer the company for the benefit of all of our "stakeholder" groups: authors, customers, employees, investors, service providers, and the communities and environment around us.

We are grateful to the thousands of readers, authors, and other friends of the company who consider themselves to be part of the "BK Community." We hope that you, too, will join us in our mission.

A BK Life Book

This book is part of our BK Life series. BK Life books change people's lives. They help individuals improve their lives in ways that are beneficial for the families, organizations, communities, nations, and world in which they live and work. To find out more, visit **www.bk-life.com**.

Berrett–Koehler
Publishers

A community dedicated to creating
a world that works for all

Dear Reader,

Thank you for picking up this book and joining our worldwide community of Berrett-Koehler readers. We share ideas that bring positive change into people's lives, organizations, and society.

To welcome you, we'd like to offer you a free e-book. You can pick from among twelve of our bestselling books by entering the promotional code **BKP92E** here: http://www.bkconnection.com/welcome.

When you claim your free e-book, we'll also send you a copy of our e-news-letter, the *BK Communiqué*. Although you're free to unsubscribe, there are many benefits to sticking around. In every issue of our newsletter you'll find

- A free e-book
- Tips from famous authors
- Discounts on spotlight titles
- Hilarious insider publishing news
- A chance to win a prize for answering a riddle

Best of all, our readers tell us, "Your newsletter is the only one I actually read." So claim your gift today, and please stay in touch!

Sincerely,

Charlotte Ashlock
Steward of the BK Website

Questions? Comments? Contact me at bkcommunity@bkpub.com.

MIX
From responsible
sources
FSC® C113845

Certified

Corporation
bcorporation.net